Soul Search

Finding Grace through Grief

by

Diane Ranker Riesen

PITTSBURGH, PENNSYLVANIA 15238

The contents of this work including, but not limited to, the accuracy of events, people, and places depicted; opinions expressed; permission to use previously published materials included; and any advice given or actions advocated are solely the responsibility of the author, who assumes all liability for said work and indemnifies the publisher against any claims stemming from publication of the work.

All Rights Reserved
Copyright © 2019 by Diane Ranker Riesen

No part of this book may be reproduced or transmitted, downloaded, distributed, reverse engineered, or stored in or introduced into any information storage and retrieval system, in any form or by any means, including photocopying and recording, whether electronic or mechanical, now known or hereinafter invented without permission in writing from the publisher.

RoseDog Books
585 Alpha Drive, Suite 103
Pittsburgh, PA 15238
Visit our website at *www.rosedogbookstore.com*

ISBN: 978-1-6461-0236-5
eISBN: 978-1-6461-0879-4

Soul Search
Finding Grace through Grief

A collection of Poetry to help inspire all those who are troubled, to comfort all those who are grieving, and to express the incredible gifts of having a growing 'Faith'.

Dedication

I lovingly dedicate this book to all the people who have struggled with illness, sorrow, and loss. Grief is one of the worst stages of life to have to bear. It spares no one. I can only pray that God has given me some words that will encourage you, and show you that our loved ones will always be around us.

Diane

A Feather

If you see a feather ~ pick it up... and touch your heart -
I sent that feather to you so we wouldn't feel apart.
I'll send you little prizes.... until we meet again ~
and they will show my care for you and help you through till then.

Your earthly world is not the same as where my soul stays now.....
I'm so at peace and so content ~~ I want to show you how.
So everytime you find a little treasure on your way ~~~
it's just my way of giving you a 'hug' to last the day.

A cardinal flies, a flower blooms, and stars shine bright at night.....
each special sight is just to show how much my soul's alright.
Oh there's much more for us to share and so much more to see ~
I'm waiting for the time when you can see it all with me.

Until that time, be grateful ~~ and cherish every hour......
smile at every child you see and dance in every shower ~~
The joys you'll find when you're with me are far beyond compare ~~
God's glorious beauty fills my soul ~ and you will see it there!!

Diane Ranker Riesen

A Grieving Parent

Don't ask me to get over it ~ or tell me life moves on....
don't think you know my feelings now that my sweet child is gone.
There is no time frame possible ~ the years don't change my pain ~
some days I'm feeling better- then my heartbreak comes again.

If you really want to help me… just please be there as a friend -
my life is changed forever - and it won't be 'fine' again.
I understand you want to help ~ there's not much you can do…
just hug me and be 'silent'- that one hug will help me through.

Advice is just not helpful - though you think you're being 'kind'...
just love me as I am right now… my path is 'mine' to find.
Unless you've lost a child yourself ~ don't think that I am weak.....
and even then you cannot know ~ for each grief is 'unique'.

My life will still continue and great joys will come my way ~
but this loss is now a part of me - it's different every day.
Please understand I know you care - you want 'ME' back the same.....
but I'll never be that person now… and never will 'again'.

Just say a prayer and love me.... let me grieve as I must do -
I'll be forever grateful ~ your support will help me through.
Grief will last forever ~~~ and you 'must' accept it's true....
just love me as I am now and I'll love and cherish 'you'.

Diane Ranker Riesen

A Peek

Have you ever noticed something small…. that takes your breath away?
I saw something quite simple ~~ that made me cry today.
I took my daily morning walk while people passed me by ---
and a glance at someone's haircut made me stop and start to cry.

For one split second I was shocked… and thought I saw you there…..
it was the special color ~~~ and the same style as YOUR hair.
I felt the urge to run to you… my heart was beating fast ~~~~
reality took over ~~ and that feeling didn't last.

It's happened many times before ~~ when I would least expect….
I'd hear a voice that stunned me…or a scent that I'd detect --
and suddenly someone I lost just seemed to be so near ~~~~
and I, for one split second… could pretend that they were here.

I miss my loved ones dearly ~ there are days I feel so weak….
that I would offer all I own --- to simply get a 'peek' -
but memories need to do for now ~ and dreams can help me, too……
until that perfect moment when I'm back again with you!

Diane Ranker Riesen

Alive

From out a dark and sealed up tomb ---
Christ our Savior left the room…..
His body walked and they could see ~~
He rose from death upon that tree.

What wondrous joy to see His face -
and know our sins could be erased ~~~
a gift so pure - a love so true…..
Christ rose again… for me… for you!

Diane Ranker Riesen

All that Matters

Give me words O Lord I pray ~~~
to thank you for my life today.
Keep me grounded in your plan…
avoiding all the traps of 'man'.

Nothing really matters ~
each night the sun has set..
but the deeds I've done to honor you;
the rest I can forget.

Help me even more, Lord ~
when I wake up in the morn…
to do the things You've meant me to
since the moment I was born.

For in the end when time stands still…
and our earth turns no more ~~
all that really matter…..
        is the truths that I stood for.

Diane Ranker Riesen

Alzheimer Loss

Slowly, very slowly ~ ever softly you erase....
I see the vagueness in your eyes - and loss upon your face.
I knew that I was losing such a major part of you ~ ~
and struggled as each month progressed .. on what my heart could do.

'Alzheimers' steals a perfect mind and holds an evil power...
Your loved ones slowly back away - and things change every hour.
But 'nothing' can take love away.... no illness can decay --
all the joy and memories that everyone has made.

As all the thoughts get weaker ~ and the illness steals their dreams....
You vow to always show your love to them by any means.
Those ending years are heartless; and it tears strong at your soul ~
it's at these times, one starts to wonder what their loved one knows.

Were they aware of all my love; and how I dearly cared?
Do they still remember memories we had when I was there?
I know God has them stored somewhere ~ in a very special place,
and when we get to Heaven ~ we'll replay them face-to-face.

And I will know you felt it all... and knew the love we shared -
together we can then relive all the special hours we cared.
'Forever' will be endless ~ what a mighty dream come true....
I'll get to have you back again... a 'whole' and perfect YOU!

Diane Ranker Riesen

Angels Sing?

I heard a story long ago ~ it stayed within my thoughts....
it caused me many questions... and such 'answers' I have sought.
The story claimed that angels sing whenever someone dies ~
and that confused me endlessly... I felt they should have cried.

I'd hear kind thoughts from people...when one I loved was gone;
and when they said that Heaven smiled ~ I felt it was so 'wrong'.
How could there be such joy around... and how could it be true?
All I felt was sadness and deep grief when I lost you?

I was so young and unaware... I wept and felt 'alone' ~
many people bothered me when happiness was shown.
There can't be any reason why the Heavens would rejoice...
I'd never see my friends again ~ I'd never hear their voice.

One night as I lay restless... I left bed and hit my knees ~
I sensed that God was calling me - to answer what I'd need.
Suddenly I felt a rush of warm air by my bed ~
while quietly I listened, ... this is what my "Father" said.

"Dear child, I've heard your questions ~ and I understand your pain...
How could the sad loss that you feel   be part of Heaven's 'gain'?
Faith takes time to comprehend what happens when one dies ~
you miss them here on earth for now... but oh their spirit flies!

Grief will come with each new loss ~ and faith can't stop this pain...
but with God's help and constant power - you'll comprehend the "gain".
For death is only temporary ~ spirits never die ~
they move to a much better place where no one ever cries.

God let me feel a tiny touch of what the angels see ~
and why they sing in joyful praise when spirit's are set free.
My lost ones are not really gone ~ they've just moved to a place….
where they will live eternally in such amazing 'grace'!

Diane Ranker Riesen

Anger

Oh, Lord, I've been so bad today ~
I let my anger guide my way...
I know it's wrong; it wasn't meant,
but sometimes I just have to vent.

I know You're listening to me...
and You care about my pleas.
But when I feel unanswered ~
I forget to hit my knees.
I know Your timing isn't my time; and I don't understand...
I pray and then expect to feel some change within Your Hand.
I've got to quit demanding that my prayers are answered fast ~
You know the way to do it; so the answers really last.

I'm sorry, Lord, today was wrong ~
I have some days like this;
but deep inside my troubled soul...
I know that You exist.
I'll try a little harder; and approach Your throne in peace ~
if I fill up my soul with You ~ my anger will decrease.

Diane Ranker Riesen

Another Dusk

Another dusk ……... the sun has set ~
the moon glows soft as evening lets
me have some time
as night sneaks through..
for me to spend some time with You.

I use some pause to clear my mind….
to slow my thoughts so I can find ~
the words to send You perfect prayer..
in total Faith- I know You're there.

Thank you Lord for these sweet hours ~
the miracles shown… the perfect flowers….
each child that passed me on my way;
and made this such a perfect day.

I pray I've found a way to show…
the love You've caused my soul to know -
and lived the hours in such a way…
that people sought Your Face today!

Diane Ranker Riesen

As Darkness Settles

As darkness settles in.... and all my senses gently slow ~
I sit in quiet stillness and watch the starlights grow.
What beauty lies within this time ~ when everything's at rest....
I think upon the beauty and know that I am "blessed".

Oh tender night be sweet to me ~ fill my soul with peace -
let my inner happiness bring forth such sweet release.
And Lord, how thankful my heart feels ~ to see You everywhere....
How blessed it is to know that I can find You ANYWHERE!!!

Diane Ranker Riesen

Babies Again

Please let me have my babies back ~
the way they were at first...
my arms are cold and lonely;
and I have that 'mothers' thirst.

Just to see their tiny fingers -
gently in my hand ~~
I know that any mother
can surely understand!

Those angel eyes that open softly -
when they wake up in the morn...
I want some moments with them ~
like when they first were born.

That 'baby' smell that fills the room...
reaches to my soul ~
it was those precious times with them -
when I felt truly 'whole'.

I loved their years of growing up....
and adored them at each stage ~
but sometimes for one moment more -
I want that 'infant' age.

Every look and every smile is safe within my mind -
I wouldn't trade the years we've shared... for any other kind.
But oh those newborn moments -- are stored within my soul ~
and when I really need them ~ I know just where to go.

Diane Ranker Riesen

Before My Sleep

Darkness waits for no one ~~~ the sky will lose it's light....
it's nature's simple signal now to settle for the night.
Before you slip to slumber - I pray your day was full
and you accomplished something to help somebody's soul.

For each day is a trial... and we have the choice to choose -
exactly how you treat each hour and how your day is used.
I pray tonight we feel content in how we spent our day ~~
in how we nurtured kindness and loved along the way.

Help me God to always use each day the way You wish....
and notice every miracle, each smile, and baby's kiss.
Tomorrow is wide open...please direct the plans I make ~~
then I can feel content and safe.. until my eyes awake.

Diane Ranker Riesen

Billowed Clouds

Such luminous clouds amid the skies ~
God's perfection... makes me cry.
An entrance to sweet Heaven's door...
just a view of so much more!

Those billowed mounds of beauty...
such glorious sights to see ~
they make me smile and dream for hours -
seen softly through the sun and showers.

Some day I wish to see them close...
one gift from God.. I love the most.
I can't imagine what's in store ~
the day I enter Heaven's door.

I daily take the time to view ~
the great creations God can do....
And then when my earth's time will end -
I'll see much more of God.... my friend!

Diane Ranker Riesen

BIRTHDAY, ONE DAY

Another year has slowly past~
and I still ache... just like the last.
I still can't celebrate your day...
no birthday presents ready ~
and nothing I can say.

I wish God gave me this one time-
to shower you with love.
I'm certain angels sing you songs...
but I'm not there ~~~~ above.

Some days just seem much harder;
although each~ has worn my heart.
I never dreamed this day would dawn~
with you and me apart.

But I will trust God's words of truth...
and try to sense your joy.
I pray You feel such happiness
upon your birthday morn—
and know my soul was blessed by God
the day that you were born.

My memories and the love we shared~
will ease me through today ....
until I get to spend the hours ~~~~
in Heaven ... on this day.

Diane Ranker Riesen

Blessed Heaven

Sometimes Heaven comes real close ~ although I'm still on earth....
it sneaks up to me in the quiet - and comforts with such worth.
It could be just an ordinary, simple, easy day......
but then my heart is changed in an extraordinary way!

Suddenly I feel the need to help someone in need ~
or reach out in a simple way and plant a soulful seed.
My mind is cleared of troubles - and my heart is beating clear.....
it's obvious a miracle is lingering very near.

Oh I love those moments... what wondrous gifts I keep-
I'm happier than ever even though I start to weep.
I'm anxious to see Heaven ~ what wonders can't be known....
but one day .. saved by Jesus' love- I know that I'll be shown.

Diane Ranker Riesen

Blessings

Tonight before I lay to rest ~ and bid today good-bye….
I want to thank God for His love; and want to tell Him 'why'.
There's nothing that can ever be - as marvelous as 'HE"…..
who gives me breath to live each day and takes good care of me.

I tend to sometimes disregard the many gifts He shares..
And all the countless moments that show how much He cares.
Nothing would be possible…. all things would disappear ~
without His Mighty Power and all He gives us here.

Thank you God.. for mercies shown ~ for all my soul receives.
I can't imagine all that waits for those here who 'believe'….
Until I get to Heaven… until I see Your face ~~~~
I'm thankful that I see YOUR touch and power every place!

Diane Ranker Riesen

Blind Faith

If I close my eyes so very tight ~ and pray real hard to You.....
Would You help me know for certain? Is there something You can do?
I'm missing loved ones terribly and though You're in my soul ~
I want more proof that Heaven's real.... I really need to know.

"My child, these times of doubt will come ~ and I do understand....
your view is very limited and swayed by laws of man.
The doubts you have are normal ~ and I know they'll come to you ~
your vision is quite limited.... I have a different view.

Hold tight onto My promises and fill your soul with prayer.
This quiet, sacred time will help you feel your loved ones there.
Blind faith can be so daunting~~ and you often question 'why';
but every time you feel alone... remember ~ "I don't lie".

My words are truthful, strong, and real ~ hold tightly to My hand.
You'll be rewarded one day .. and it's then you'll understand.
My Ways are far beyond your mind ~ on earth you'll never feel..
the kind of 'proof' you're searching for ~ but one day, it comes real.

I'll send you little signs of truth ~ and help you make it through...
until I call you home to stay.......
                          and all your dreams come true!"

Diane Ranker Riesen

Blooms

What joyous sight to look outside and see the blooming flowers ~
the beauty fills my heart with peace and I could watch for hours.
Each tiny bloom is reaching out and starting strong to grow....
no one on earth can recreate.... for only God can know.

God's power shines in every bloom; and all HIs love is seen...
the stunning hues of petals and each perfect sight of green.
And as they stretch up from the ground ~ they reach up to the sky....
their fragrance permeates the air and I begin to cry.

How awesome is our mighty God.. that He would take the time ~
to give us all this beauty.. these gifts are yours and mine.
Each moment that I walk amongst these miracles ~ I see...
that God is living in each flower ~ His boundless gifts are free.

Today I'll take a walk outside ~ and see the flowers up close...
I couldn't pick a favorite..... I love them ALL the most.
Take the time to study every bloom that comes to sight ~
and use each sign of beauty.. to witness God's great 'might'!

Diane Ranker Riesen

Childhood Tree

Up high upon the tallest branch of our old willow tree ~
I climbed and sat to look around; and find what I could see.
No one noticed I was there, while all the neighbors played ~
I thought it would be fun to watch, so I sat still and stayed.

A couple houses down from us.. some neighbor boys played ball-
and from my perfect vantage point ~~ I could see it all.
As each boy took his turn to bat…. I saw their anxious stance~
when one boy hit a home run ~ I watched his victory dance!

Some girls were outside swinging, as some new ones came along…
and as they swung so high and fast ~ I heard their giggling song.
I turned around and saw some Springtime bunnies hopping slow ~
and then, they scurried to their nest. They sensed me near, I know.

It was such a peaceful feeling ~~ just resting in that tree;
where I could notice all the things that others could not see.
There's so much life going on each day ~ I seldom took the time…
to slow myself completely down, and see what I could find.

I still remember sitting there, although the years have past.
Certain times are precious and their memories always last.
So many sweet thoughts come to mind; that I did long ago.
It's times like this that I look back, and miss my childhood 'so'.

We all still need to take a breath; and lean back to observe ~
And soak in all the joyful things… the trees, the skies, the birds.
There's so much more to notice ~ if we only took the time….
and this one childhood memory will always be "just mine".

Diane Ranker Riesen

Christmas Truth

Can we keep the Christmas spirit ~ keep it all year long?
What a joyful world we'd have if we could always hold it strong.
There's just a magic in the air ~ like Heaven's come down close....
our hearts just want to love as if we have an extra dose.

Oh glorious lights that line the streets and signs of Christmas Peace~
the world seems blessed with extra joy, and hatred tends to cease.
Sweet carollers begin their rounds, and sing such happy praise....
Hot chocolate warms their bellies~ as their lovely voices 'raise'.

Cuddled down before a fire ~ with velvet blankets close....
I think those special evenings are the times I love the most.
We think more joy, we see more love, and softness fills our souls ~
The magic time when Christmas looms - has power never known.

With all the fun, the gifts, and cards ~ they never can compare......
to Christmas morn when Christ is born, and Angels saw Him there!
A tiny babe to save our world ~ a child who would be King ~~~
Who'll change the course of every sin; and conquer everything.

Enjoy this perfect Season ~ smile at those you see......
hug your friends and family; and spread your kindness 'free' ~
but always keep Christ's birth secure; and stored within your heart.....
without His selfless sacrifice ... no holiday would start!

Diane Ranker Riesen

Claim Him

Don't let such evils get you ~ don't let the bad guys win…
wrap God's strength around you….before your day begins.
This world can knock you to your knees, and try to steal your 'joy',
but God has greater plans for you ~ just trust Him and 'enjoy'.

Have God wrap His arms around you - soon as you awake….
and face the day with strengthened power…so you will never break.
And when the worst of circumstances hover round you close ~
remember who is Mightier …. and trust His power the most.

We are the children of a King ~ the Healer of our pains;
Who whispers and controls the world.. He'll help us once again.
May His power guard your day and comfort every trial…
and may we be content to know He's with us all the while.

Step out into your new day ~ and claim your Maker's power;
find such relief in knowing that He's with you every hour.
The evils of this world will lose much power over you ~
if you claim God's great Mightiness…. in everything you do.

Diane Ranker Riesen

Colored Glory

Oh, how I love the crisp cool breeze of Autumn on my skin ~
the multitude of colors that invade each tree begins.
I love the sound of crunching leaves beneath each step I take ~
each day brings forth more changes- with each miracle God makes.

The squirrels begin to store up all their acorns for the cold…..
as they scurry up into the trees of crimson, brown, and gold.
I watch so many birds take flight in such a perfect form ~
their instinct tells them where to fly and migrate somewhere warm.

It's magical what happens when each Summer goes to rest….
each season is so perfect ~ I can't say which one is best.
I look forward to the Autumn with it's bonfires burning bright ~
as I sit around the fire ….. and see all the sights of night.

Oh, Fall, how perfect can you be? ….God's "work" in stunning show ~
with all the changing colors and much more we cannot know.
God's earth is such a miracle ~ His timing in each view -
I stand amazed in wonder… nature proves that God is 'true'!

Diane Ranker Riesen

Constant Memories

Constant memories linger close.....
the kind that always mean the most -
of days long gone when we were young;
and all our world had just begun.

On the swing set we would be.....
just singing while we felt so free ~
and then we'd walk down to the park;
and run home quick when it was dark.

Those simple times will never leave....
the best in life ~~ I do believe.
When all the world seemed nice and right -
and every dream could just take flight.

Sometimes now, when I'm feeling low ~
I think back on those years I know;
and all that innocence returns...
the simple 'love' our hearts would learn.

Don't ever let those memories fade ~
we'll use them when we feel afraid.....
that all the world is changing fast.
We'll dream about our happy past.

Although the world will always change...
and easy times will rearrange -
Our minds can go back to those years...
and help the good days reappear.

Diane Ranker Riesen

Constant

Why do I wonder constantly?...the night time makes it worse.....
Unnecessary worry is a never-ending curse.
It really serves no purpose - just a cause of endless sleep....
I've always known it's useless ~ yet, it's something I still keep.

They say that it's like 'rocking'... you keep going; but get nowhere.
It's a waste of boundless energy ~ yet I still don't seem to care.
It's wrong to hold these burdens - but, my worries never cease ---
I've tried to stop so many times.... It's such a strong disease.

God's the only answer, and I pray to Him each night ~
I ask His Power to help me....knowing 'worry' is not right.
I know God hears my countless prayers ~ He wants to set me 'free'......
Please help me to remember ~ He'll take this pain from me.

I have to try much harder ~ my faith must firmly stand....
and when I start to worry ~ I must place it in God's Hands.
Each time my mind gets clouded...and I start to worry more ~
I need to give it all to God ~ ~ for HE will understand.

Diane Ranker Riesen

Creation

One day I hope to see the world ~ the way it first began.
Created in perfection... before the birth of man ~
when everything was bright and new; the skies were fresh and clear...
I truly can't imagine all the beauty God brought here.

The waters shown of aqua blue ~ and fresh with gorgeous views....
A rainbow sent to bless our world with reds, and greens, and blues.
The grass laid out like carpet... as it swayed within the breeze ~
so many wondrous miracles ~ and many more of these.

With all this mighty beauty ~~~~ God knew it would not stay;
for man was born and sent to earth - and then 'sin' had its way.
Carelessness and greed were seen where once the world was pure ~
the perfect beauty newly born - had much it would endure.

But I will see it new again ~ one day when God returns...
and, hopefully by then, a new found thankfulness is learned.
What stunning sights my eyes will see... with no more pain or fear ~
a perfect world awaiting us when God's glory reappears!

Diane Ranker Riesen

Daily Joy

I see dreams in every flower -
and long to dance in every shower.
The sunshine sends me strands of gold ~
and moonbeams give me peace to hold.

I believe in dreams come true…
and hope sweet angels follow you.
I see such hope in every eye ~
see their sparks, and never cry.

Every tree can sing a song …
whistling breeze where nothing's wrong.
What a world if all could hear ---
every melody lingering near.

Babies make my heart beat strong ~
those perfect souls are never wrong.
I wish each person got to see….
all God's gifts surrounding me.

Take some time, and breathe in deep ~
grab each moment you can keep.
The years fly by, too soon all gone…..
enjoy this world where you belong!

Diane Ranker Riesen

Daily Remembrance

Why does it seem so easy when your life is going well ~
to forget the 'One' who brings you breath, and forget to pray and tell...
how much you love Him daily and are grateful for His Power?
Without God we would be so lost, within each single hour.

And yet, I know God understands ~ His mercy overflows....
He wants us to be happy; and deep inside He knows -
how much our Faith controls our day and gives us hope when lost;
He knows we still remember Him, and love at any cost.

But I still want to try my best to keep Him first in mind ~
and always thank His 'leading' me, and always help me find..
Thank you God, though I forget, just how you fill my life ~~
how great Your Power comforts me when I am torn with strife.

You are my King, my Majesty ~ and though, I often fall ~~
YOU are the reason I survive; and love You.. most of all!

Diane Ranker Riesen

Dark

Have you ever been so tired ~ even though you need no sleep;
the pressures all around you have you swimming in the deep?
I've had those times when every hour has torn me to the core ~
and I feel so lost and hopeless that I just can't take no more.

The world is filled with sorrow ~ and your heart is torn with pain....
your only hope is taking time to step out of the rain.
There'll always be a new day that's just waiting round the bend ~
and with your strength and faith intact... your troubled times will end.

Don't let the world take hold of all the blessings God has sent -
Don't let the hopeless feelings cause your spirit to be spent.
God stands above each sorrow ~ and earth trembles at His hand....
just close your eyes and lean on Him--- His power will help you stand.

You cannot be defeated; nor your life be so confused....
It's in your power - with hope and prayer - to not be so abused.
Those deep and dark times lurking .. will always find a way ~
to weaken all your senses and try to wreck the day.

Your tiredness will be refreshed when you fall to your knees.....
bow your head in reverence; and then give to God your pleas.
No matter what your pain is   God will always send you peace ~
and you'll get through those darkened days with help from God's release.

Diane Ranker Riesen

December Birth

I feel December's breeze blow near ~
such a Holy Time we have each year ..
when God prepared to bring His Son ~
to save our souls when He is done.

Bright lights begin to fill the air ~
and Christmas cheer is everywhere!
Bells and songs ~ with happy glee…
and wrapped up presents by the tree.

But though this makes 'December' fun …
we must rejoice the Holy One ~
the Christ Child soon to enter life…
amid a stable filled with strife.

No luxuries for our newborn King ~
no warmth ~ and yet, the Angels sing!
Rejoice…. Our future is secured -
sweet songs from Heaven can be heard.

Enjoy this month of endless joys …
with all the merriment and toys ~
but always praise the greatest 'Worth' -
the Son of God's miraculous birth!

Diane Ranker Riesen

Decisions

Oh, this day's been full of trials ~
let me rest here ~ for awhile…..
I pray I made no huge mistakes -
grant me peace before I wake.

When I lift my doubts to You ~
and pray You'll show me what to do…..
then all my fears should disappear ----
I gave my choice, for You to hear.

Thank you, Lord, for tender peace
knowing I can then 'release',
any fear that I may face ~
I'll put assurance in its place.

For You, alone, rule over all ~
You'll save and catch me when I fall…..
and with Your Power all worries fade -
Decisions ''in Your name'' were made.

Diane Ranker Riesen

Divine Sky

So softly dims the sunlight's view ~
as the sky shows forth such stunning hues.
Colors changing by the hour…
as perfect as the sight of flowers.

God bids farewell to one more day -
with this miraculous, sweet display.
This evening brings a brand new scene ~
of oranges, purples, pinks, and greens.

I love God's painting hanging there….
across the slowly, darkening air.
And in the morn… new light will shine ~
God's divine gift that's yours and mine!

Diane Ranker Riesen

Do It!

Take a walk and jump a rope -
smell the flowers ~ grab some hope....
Send a smile to all you see -
share your joy and just be free!

Life is filled with wonders;
so many perfect hours ~~
Create some angels in the snow;
and dance within the showers!

Find some love each morning,
each day and every night -
and relish all the beauty
that shines within your sight.

Sorrows try to capture us ~
don't let them stay for long...
"Happiness" can conquer them ---
For LOVE is very STRONG!

Diane Ranker Riesen

Dreams of Heaven

Let's have a dream of Heaven ~ let's see what we can find....
Let's pray before... that God lets us have glimpses in our mind.
I've heard descriptions many times... and read the Bible's view ~
People claim to shortly die, return.. and say "It's True"!

The one thing that I surely know is that our dreams would pale
in comparison to what we'll see - any 'look' will fail.
But just imagine viewing just a bit of what we'll see......
when earthly time is over; and we're in ETERNITY!

A mesmerizing picture of a peaceful, perfect place ~~
with unknown colors filling up within this Holy Space.
I imagine soft, sweet music blowing through the gorgeous trees....
and the loving scent of flowers floating tender in the breeze.

All my loved ones gone before.... just smiling in the light ~
and feeling deep within my soul that everything is 'right'.
The meadows, streams, and butterflies are glistening everywhere....
and every thought I hoped for ~ was even better there.

Then, just when I could not imagine any beauty more ~~~~
I feel a presence walk towards me - that warms me to my core.
My Father, God, holds out His arms - and welcomes me with grace...
I burst with tears of happiness ~ as I look upon His Face.

I think a dream could show me... just a tiny, little view ~
but nothing could compare to when I finally come to 'You'.
My earthly eyes could never bear the brilliance so serene --
Heaven will display much more than I could ever dream!

Diane Ranker Riesen

Dreams

How can dreams appear so real ~ and deeply touch my heart?.....
I pray before I fall asleep and hope sweet thoughts will start.
For in this dark and silent space... my mind can wander free ~
and often in the morning - a dream has rescued me.

In frozen time I travel free, and dance among the clouds...
I say the words I need to say ~ but, never say out loud.
I'm visited so often in my dreams by people gone ~
and I don't feel so lonely ~ and things don't seem so wrong.

Sometimes a day will seem so hard ~ I can't wait for the night....
when I can dream my wishes, and my light soul can take flight.
These special dreams can comfort me.... when nothing else compares ~
they give a chance for me to smile and steal me from my cares.

Oh, dreams of silent night be strong... and, lift my soul to peace ~
give me special hours~~~~ for my hurts to feel release.
Sometimes a dream can change my view and show me how to cope...
when morning hours awaken me .... I feel some new found 'hope'.

Diane Ranker Riesen

Dusk

As evening slowly comes to view and nature ends it's day ~
the earth responds in poignant moves; and creatures have their way.
The large and looming willow trees bend down to lay their head....
while all the gorgeous flowers curl up tight to go to bed.

Each rabbit nestled softly and together in their nest....
while all the stately deers and does look 'round to find some rest.
The sun slides slowly out of sight and coolness hits the air ~~
as all the sunshine disappears and dark is everywhere.

Tiny crickets sing a tune to bid the day farewell....
the ocean tides all follow true; as waves no longer swell.
A sense of quiet calmness seems to cover all the land ~
I feel God's grace surrounding me; and now I understand.

God's beauty shows forth endlessly... at any given hour.
The moonbeams send soft strands of light and frame a tiny flower.
Perfection shows in all God's works; as I stand struck in awe ~
God's power lives each moment ..in the beauties that I saw.

And now, I choose to bid farewell; and lay down for the night...
while angels hover 'round the skies and nightly owls take flight.
Oh, how I love each moment ~ every differing time of day....
no matter when I choose to hear... God has so much to say!

Diane Ranker Riesen

Each Day

When my years have come and gone ~ when all my time is spent.....
I never want to worry what I missed or where they went.
Our time is very precious.. and the years fly by so fast ~~~~
I pray I spent the hours doing something that will last.

We all can make a difference ~~~ each person has the power....
to brighten up somebody's life and spread love every hour.
It doesn't need to take great strength to make a simple change ~
God's always had a plan for each of us to rearrange.

Some days you may not notice.... it's so small you didn't see ~
but, you'll never know the magic that is caused by you and me.
A simple wave to someone lost ~ or just a kind 'hello'......
is much more special and can cause more change you'll ever know.

God formed you for a purpose, and He holds you in His Hands....
You'll make more perfect difference than you'll ever understand.
Just use each day for kindness... forgive each wrong, and pray ~
then you can rest in perfect peace when ending every day.

Diane Ranker Riesen

Empathy

We need such strength to carry on when everything seems wrong ~
You feel so lost and stranded in a place you don't belong.
Such trials in life are daunting ~ and so hard to comprehend....
Each pain is real to those it hits... and we must understand.

There are so many people who feel countless trials every day -
and we must learn to understand, and help them in some way.
Perhaps it's just a listening ear ~ and they just need to know....
that kindness can be found in friends; when there's no place to go.

I believe that 'empathy' should never be denied...
this show of love and caring can reverse and change the tide.
Everyone needs help at times; a heart just needs some care ~
it's priceless knowing when you're down .. that someone else is there!

Don't be afraid to stretch your arms- and reach out to a friend....
so many hurts are helped by love, and YOU can help pain 'end'.
We can't control the trials of life ~ hard times will touch us all ~~
but we can help each other... acts of love will catch the 'fall'.

I want to try with every breath ~~ to be a helping hand....
and give hope to the weary, and help them understand ......
that when they need some extra strength, and need a little 'care' ~
they can merely ask in prayer, and someone will be there!

Diane Ranker Riesen

Eve

Oh, how softly creeps the night time ~
with such softened, quiet sounds.....
Every shadow wraps around you-
as less sunlight can be found.

All of nature nestles down...
to find a place to rest and slumber.
The tiny creatures out of sight ~
no longer seen; but hiding under.

Soft, whispered sounds of evening hours ~
find a way to calm my soul -
as I'm homebound for the day....
with all the sights that made it full.

One more glance outside my window ~
I look to gaze upon the moon....
knowing that within short hours ---
another day will waken soon.

Diane Ranker Riesen

Evening Flight

Can I take an evening flight....
and touch each star within the night?
Can I soar beyond the trees....
and smell the sweetness of the breeze?

Perhaps I'll do this in a dream ~
amid the clouds of white and cream....
I'll see the view from way up high -
and notice miracles from the sky!

What perfect peace ~ what gentle show....
for me to sense.... for me to know ~~
how truly perfect our world seems -
within my secret night time dream.

Diane Ranker Riesen

Ever Surely

Softly, ever surely comes the music of the night ~
a million tiny evening bugs whose wings are taking flight.
The crickets chirp a lullaby around the lily pond....
and cause such songs of glory... as heaven waves it's wand.

A bull frog splashes water as he leaps from stone to stone ~
I love each melody I hear... I love each subtle tone.
What joy my heart feels everytime - I stand out in the night;
and gaze my view on every perfect miracle in sight.

The evening is my quiet friend ~ it always soothes my soul....
my mind is clear, my heart beats soft, and I feel really whole.
Take a walk into the night and hear the songs it sings ~
and in those special moments.. cherish all the joy it brings!

Diane Ranker Riesen

Eyes of a Child

I remember hearing of this when I wasn't very old ~
it's become one of the favorite tales I ever have been told.
My mom would always sit me 'neath the Christmas tree and start.....
the words would always touch me and I've stored them in my heart.

She told me of a young boy who I've never met or known -
who showed what Christmas Love's about - so little, on his own.
Each year his family went and picked a gorgeous Christmas tree ~
and he would love to see the lights ~ how special it would be.

He looked outside his window on one morn, the cold was bad...
and saw a tiny balsam tree ~ it made him very sad.
It stood alone and seemed so small; and then, he saw His tree.
He scurried down the steps; and from his lips came this soft plea ~

"Mom, can we bring it inside? It seems so sad to me....
that everyone has Christmas trees inside, so warm, you see.
My heart feels sad that tree's so small; and looks so all alone ~
can we bring it inside with us?"
.. and he began to moan.

His mother told him of God's plan and that all trees start small ~
they need to be outside to grow, and then grow very tall.
My sweet boy, it's so hard to see ~ but trust that God knows best..
and years from now, you'll see it's strength and understand the rest.

He listened to his mother's words; but, still felt slightly torn....
so he decided Christmas time is all about that morn' ~~~~
when baby Jesus came to earth... when 'Love' was truly born.

Diane Ranker Riesen

That night he looked around his room; and searched his heart to find~
a way that he could show God's love ~ a way he could be kind.
The next day when his mother woke - she looked outside ...... to see;
her little boy had wrapped his favorite blanket 'round that tree.

She suddenly felt soft, warm tears stream down her joyful face ....
her little boy had gifted her with signs of 'Christmas Grace'.
"Did you see what I did late last night before I went to bed?
I think God will be glad I helped to warm that tree.", he said.

Diane Ranker Riesen

Eyes of Heaven

Sometimes, Heaven seems to hide…. it seems to be asleep ~~
It doesn't seem to notice when you're hurting, or you weep.
Our sorrows seem to shadow all the light that Heaven sends….
our troubles seem to blind us, and we just can't seem to mend.

But Heaven's filled with only 'love' ---- it's never harsh or mean ~
It's waiting for our simple trust ~~~ and longing to be seen.
Our world is torn and broken… and great tragedies occur -
but I was touched by God's great love, and Heaven's 'real' for sure.

My soul was overwhelmed today…. my pain was blinding me ~
but God sent me a gift of joy ~ and caused my eyes to see.
There are these special moments that reach down and touch your soul…..
then suddenly your doubts are cured - - and broken hearts are whole.

I met a special baby…. who comforted my grief ----
and, even though much pain occurs- I got such great relief.
I saw Heaven so clearly --- behind this baby's eyes ~
down deep behind this outward sight… it's beauty made me cry.

This sweet child looked right at me … and time stood softly 'still'-
I can't forget the beauty, and I know I never will.
I learned that Heaven's always near ~ it waits in every soul ----
We need to take the time to 'SEE'… I felt it there, I know.

I thank God for this meeting… God knew I needed peace ~
within those eyes I saw such love, and I received relief.
I realized God is always close ~ He understands our pain….
but when I seem to falter…. God will prove HImself again.

Diane Ranker Riesen

Fluttering Glory

So many gorgeous butterflies ~ I see them everywhere.....
they land upon the flowers and flutter in the air.
I find myself enthralled by them, and love to sit and see ~
these beautiful creations dancing soft.. surrounding me.

No two are ever quite the same ~ those wings of glorious hues...
from soft and pastel pinks and cream... to bright and joyous blues.
Their colors still amaze me and I view them each in awe ~
so exquisitely created.... without a single flaw.

Perhaps they're bits of heaven ~ that visit us each day....
to brighten up our afternoons, and dance within our way.
The butterflies on earth are so miraculous to see ~
I can't imagine Heaven's unknown colors there will be.

If God can put such beauty in such tiny things as these....
imagine all the stunning sights in 'glory' we will see.
So perfectly designed in love ~ with wings of countless hues ~
will pale compared to all the ones in Heaven we will view!

Diane Ranker Riesen

Gentle Evening

So gently blows the evening breeze ~
in quiet tune with rustling leaves -
Every songbird takes its rest..
And slumbers quiet in its nest.

Daytime noise has disappeared -
all the problems… all the fears ~
Each night calls our hearts to rest….
and dwell on how we're loved and blest.

No more worries are allowed ~
on bended knee with forehead bowed….
Prayers sent upward for the night -
Release your sins, and feel God's 'light'.

Then in humble praise retire …..
as each new dream is lifted higher ~
And night's sweet rest restores your soul -
Then with dawn's light you're new and whole.

Every dawn brings more to view ….
use each hour ~ feel all that's new ~
Then when your day comes to its end -
You'll have the night to rest 'again'.

Diane Ranker Riesen

Gifts

What sweet gifts our Lord has given ….
such a glorious world to live in -
Amazing nature sings its songs ~
and we see miracles all day long!

Hello, sweet birds… who soar the skies ~
with wings from God that let them fly…..
Such peaceful beauty you display..
through every hour - through every day.

I watched a rose unfold its face ~
such perfect timing - glorious grace….
God's timed each season perfectly -
they give me so much joy to see.

The flowers, trees, the clouds and sky ~
all shine such beauty to my eyes….
What a gracious God ~ right from the start ---
You've blessed us all… how great Thou art!

Diane Ranker Riesen

God's Helpers

My Child, there are some special things I have for you to do....
although, I know the sadnesses and trials that you've been through.
You've been changed by these great sorrows, and you need to let more know -
that your Faith has helped you conquer them... and it's time for YOU to 'show'!

Let others know your heart was broken ~ ~ let them feel your pain;
with the witness from your strengthened soul... they'll see there's HOPE again.
Your purpose is a special one - all the Heavens bless your days ~~~
so many other people will be strong by things you say.

Just as My Son bore sorrows on that Cross so long ago....
Your heartaches taught you 'mercy'.. other people need to know ~~
that though great sorrows come to them.... at such a heavy cost....
each suffering they encountered... has a purpose that's not 'lost'.

God allows such heartache sometimes; and we just don't understand ~
why He won't stop them coming... with a flicker of His Hand.
God's vision is not limited to what WE have on earth....
He sees how you can help Him; and He knows your sorrows "worth".

For earth time is not HEAVEN ~ we are here just for a 'time'....
our real world lies before us - after death... in the Divine!
Use the truths your heart has learned - from every pain endured...
tell others of God's faithfulness.. tell others of His word.

You're someone very special... and your purpose will be clear ~
when you spend time with God in prayer --- just listen and you'll 'hear'...
all the special reasons why you've lived your life this way -
and you'll be blessed so richly.. for each truth your soul will say!

Diane Ranker Riesen

God's Way

The night has come, and all is still ~
I pray, today, I did God's Will.
It's hard sometimes to know the way…..
your 'spirit' feels what God would say.

Whenever there are choices…
when decisions must be made ~
choose the truth that comes to you
once you have thought and prayed.

Each day can be quite different ~
and we never know His plan…
but if you give your choice to God,
He'll bless you once again.

In hard days and in better…
in sunshine and in rain ~
God gives us strength to manage,
and He'll protect the pain.

We never know His outcome….
it can sometimes seem absurd;
but when we walk in faithful trust ~
we can believe His Word.

Help me, Lord, to follow You….
And do Thy wish each day.
You've promised all things work for good ~
so I will search Your Way.

Diane Ranker Riesen

Going to Heaven

Heaven's not a place you have to try so hard to "earn"....
once you've welcomed Jesus - you will read His words and learn ~
that all the wrongs we do each day~ each done by you and me......
were taken and forgiven when Christ died upon that tree.

So often people worry that they just won't do enough-
and Heaven's just a hopeful dream ~ it's entry's very tough.
But once Christ lives within your soul and you become real close ...
you'll really 'want' to please Him ~ He's already done the most.

Living as God wants us to —- is not a hard demand....
once you really love Him, then you'll start to understand.
All constant fears of worthlessness - will clearly go away
when your soul is filled with Jesus...His crucifixion paved the way.

The moment that I realized .. I need not live in fear
that I could NEVER earn my way - the answer was so clear!
Because I truly love my God, I want to do His Will ~
and I attempt to honor Him... it's just the way I 'FEEL'.

One night as I lay resting, and I opened up my soul —-
I heard God's silent whisper say there's something I should know:

~~~~

"Dear child of mine, you need not fret.... in Heaven you will be."

And then I knew it all was true ~ Christ earned it all FOR me."

Diane Ranker Riesen

Goodbye, Again

And now we say goodbye, again ~ as each new sorrow grows...
none of us are ready ---- or prepared to let them go.
But God has always known each day, and when each time will end.
God gives us faith to 'lean on' - when we feel new grief again.

Each of us have purpose ... in a world so filled with wrong ~
but God puts every person with the people they belong.
So now we say goodbye, again ~ but celebrate their days....
in thankful joy for all the special moments that were made.

We're grateful for the times we had, and each of us were blessed∴
please know how much we loved you; as you shined like all the rest.
The gifts of love you gave away - will always stay around ~
what special memories come to mind ~ your blessings still abound.

This goodbye's not forever ~ every person has an end....
the loss we feel takes time to heal... but, never truly mends.
We say goodbye to you, today ~ may angels guide your way ~
Be happy where your spirit lives... we'll see you all one day.

Diane Ranker Riesen

Grandparents

When God designed His plans for life and all the things on earth~
I wonder if He really knew what 'grandparents' were worth?
I'm sure He did, for He knows all ~ but what a special treat...
for 'grandparents' are so much more than anyone you'll meet.

A parent's love is special; and nothing can compare ~
but grandparents are close in line, with endless love to share.
The wisdom that you learn from them is far beyond your dreams;
and the lessons that they teach you are much more than they seem.

For all your life... you'll use their words to help you through the years ~
they're a soft, sweet spot to lean on.... to grab and calm your fears.
Don't ever think their mark on you will ever go away ~
every word of love they share is something that will stay.

How blessed we are to have them... what miracles they share;
your life is changed forever by their unconditional care.
Thank you, God, for 'grandparents' .. who change the ones they touch ~
keep all their memories deep inside; they have God's special 'touch'.

Diane Ranker Riesen

Grateful Prayer

When day time starts to dwindle down; and time appears to rest ~
I find myself reflecting and remembering how I'm blessed.
Each day is so unique and new ~ adventures unprepared...
sights amaze my visions views; and sweet sounds fill the air.

Some days seem faster than the rest, while others seem so slow ~
but every day has meaning, with new lessons shown to know.
Rainy days seem quieter ~ and nature's creatures hide....
while people tend to settle down and spend their time inside.

But raindrops help me understand the rhythm of God's plan ~
nothing hydrates all the lands like steady raindrops can.
While other days, the sun shines bright and sends sweet kisses near...
my eyes see all the flowers; and God's perfect beauties here.

How blessed I am to have these days... to see such joyous sights ~
the brilliant sunlight beaming down ~ and then the calming night.
I stand amazed and grateful... that I see the works God made;
while in the parks, each bird gave song; and little children played.

I lay to rest surrendered to each gift I got to see ~
and feel such gratefulness that God would send such love to me.
I'll sleep content and satisfied that I was richly blessed
and waken with excitement to begin to see the rest!

Diane Ranker Riesen

Gratefulness

I can catch a lightening bug ~ but I can't make it light…
and I can watch a bluebird.. but can't make that bird take flight.
I can plant a garden that will bloom a glorious show ~
but only God knows how to take those seeds and make them grow.

I look at trees and marvel ~~ as they grow so strong and tall;
but only God can make them; I watch each tree in awe.
A thousand gifts in nature that may seem such little things ~
but none of us have power to make a tiny robin 'sing'!

I take God's power for granted ~ as I walk among the trees….
and feel the sun shine down on me… and feel a gentle breeze.
Everything I see each day is formed by God's great hands ~
He rules all life and nature ~ it's quite hard to understand.

The stars, the moon, the oceans vast ~ that span across the miles;
each marvelous creation… every infant, tear, and smile.
How gracious is this God of ours ~ to bless us with this life…
Who guards our hearts with mercy, and clears our way through strife.

I continue, every day, to be amazed at God's great Power ~
Who rules the universe in tune, and controls each day and hour.
I want to be more grateful ~ as I see the gifts He brings….
and thank Him for the love He sends to me through everything!

Diane Ranker Riesen

Grieving Mothers

There is a very silent mass of hearts that never beat -
a secret group of women ... who walk amongst the streets.
I'm one of those who hide my pain, and rarely do you see ..
how hard the day can be sometimes ~ and how it tortures me.

These women walk a different path ~ and live a different life..
they try to conquer challenges amid a soul of strife.
Our tears fall soft and silently when no one else is near -
the pain we've felt has changed us ... and there's not much else we fear.

A miracle was sent to us ~ and all our dreams seemed real ...
I never dreamed the kind of 'love' a mother's soul could feel.
I wish this gift had lasted and my life had stayed the same ~
but fate had other plans for me ... I search for who to blame.

I had my child so shortly and my life seems empty now -
I pray each night my world would change - and God would show me how.
I seem to make it through each day ~~ although I rarely smile...
and hold onto the 'hope' my faith will help me all the while.

No one really 'knows' us ~~ there is no way they could feel ...
the kind of pain we suffer with a heart that cannot heal.
But one day - when the sunshine ends, and all the world is through -
we'll have our babies back again ~~ our souls will be born 'new'!

Diane Ranker Riesen

Have You?

Have you ever wished that you could just wake up..and smile with ease ~
yet before your eyes have opened.... worried thoughts begin to squeeze?
There seems to be no quiet place -- or calmness in your mind.....
the more you search for peacefulness; the more stress that you find.

I try to pray and reach to God.. but noise has filled my brain ~
I know that God can hear me ~ but it seems to be in vain.
I just can't stop the chaos... unrelenting pressure builds ~
I want to try, I really do ~ but there's nothing I can feel.

Give me strength, today, again..... to make it through this pain ~
They say that sunshine always comes ~ but all I see is rain.
Help me, God, to comprehend --- Your strength can pull me through....
and though I just don't understand... I know the answer's 'YOU'.

Faith in God is easy when you see some help in sight.....
but the neverending torment makes it hard to feel it's right.
I'll keep on trying hard to wait ~ for strength You'll send to me....
and trust the truth You have the power to help my mind feel free.

Diane Ranker Riesen

Heartache

Take each heartache ~ hold it close;
for only YOU can do the most.
I pray for every painful soul…..
for You're the one to heal, I know.

Your hand can reach down from Your throne ~
and take each sorrow for Your Own!
Your mighty strength can take these pains…
and quickly stop the hurts again.

Your shoulders carry all our strifes…
and lift us to a sweet, blessed life.
We need to trust the truths You've told,
and give our worries.. no more hold!

Your timing sometimes leaves us weak ~
for it's in Your Will, the help we seek.
I cannot understand earth's pains….
but trust You till they're gone again.

Diane Ranker Riesen

Heaven

All my life I've dreamed of Heaven ~ though I love my time on earth;
If God blesses us so richly... imagine Heaven's love and worth!
I walk among God's sights each day, and find such precious views....
but earth cannot compare to Heaven ~ all it holds in unknown hues.

I love to see a gorgeous flower... as it opens for the day ~
but nothing shows the perfect colors Heaven holds along its way.
My mind tries hard to just imagine... yet I know I need to wait....
for my brain cannot fathom... all the wonders past God's gate.

I know my soul will burst with glory- as I gaze upon the views....
perfect pinks, and purest white... such colors that I never knew.
And then, beholding God Almighty ~ the One who rules each earthly sight..
how I long to see God's Heaven..eternally ~~ each day and night.

Diane Ranker Riesen

Heaven's Door

Our universe fully engulfed…
in God's unending, sacred hope ~
our fears erased up on that tree-
when God's own Son, Christ, died for me.

In a world so clearly torn…
when all HIs children's sin were born.
We need not fear eternity ~
God made His way, and now, we're free.

Take God's gift, on bended knee ~
His sacrifice was done .. you see;
and we can claim our fate secured…
because of what God's Son endured.

What joy in knowing I am safe…
no longer sealed within a grave ~~
we all will rise and live once more;
as we all enter Heaven's door!

Diane Ranker Riesen

Hello, Spring!

Hello there, little tulip ~~~ I see you reaching 'high'.......
I knew last Fall when you were gone, that you would never die.
Sometimes such beauty leaves us... but never disappears ~
they'll be another space in time when you will be right here.

Hello there, glorious roses ~~~ your petals smell so sweet.....
I'm always looking forward to that day, again, we'll meet.
God's wondrous beauty never dies... although it takes a rest ~
but wait awhile, and once again - you'll see it at its best.

Never fear when Winter comes, and so much fades away.......
new beauties will replace them ~ but they'll come back again.
Enjoy each snowflake while it lasts ~ so perfect, so unique ~
each season's filled with glories ~ enjoy them at their peak.

But now it's time for flowers ~ all the snow has gone away ~
A myriad of perfect colors thrown throughout each day.
I love to see the blooming buds... on every stem and tree......
I welcome every Springtime ~~~ that comes right back to me!

Diane Ranker Riesen

His Answer

Frustration comes to all of us when prayers seem so unheard ~
yet, deep inside, I know that God is hearing every word.
I question if I've prayed enough; and if my heart was true….
when suddenly God softly whispers……   "I already knew."

God knows our needs before we do ~ He rules the universe….
He doesn't need to hear the things that I need from Him 'first'.
And then I question 'why I pray', since God already knows ~
it's then God takes some special time to whisper in my soul.

'My Child, your prayers were never meant to tell Me all your needs….
My Spirit lingers everywhere and always intercedes ~
but that sweet time you spend with Me… in simple, tender prayer -
Brings so much love and joy to Me, by feeling you right there.

Don't worry if you pray enough, or if they're weak or strong ~
as long as you are searching Me… no prayer is ever wrong.
My answers may not always seem to be the things you planned….
but keep your faith - your questions will be answered in the end'.

Diane Ranker Riesen

His Essence

Oh, what holds the stars in place?... What calms a stormy sea?
Why do leaves lean toward the sun ~ what magic lets us breathe?
There are so many questions that keep swirling in my mind ~
Our world contains such wonders of a thousand different kinds.

There are no simple answers that could prove how things are done....
and the only way to understand ~~ is believing in 'the One'.
He simply moves HIs finger; and the clouds begin to part ~~
He blinks to keep our universe from falling all apart.

Our God cannot be put in words - HIs majesty sustains
each life within the flowers as He redirects the rains.
Such mountains loom above us; and deep valleys down below....
without the power of His Hands no life would ever grow.

Thank you, God ~ for loving us; and for Your mighty care...
Your essence is the only way that everything is here.
You paint each sunset with Your soul, and then 'light up the day' ~
There is no other answer..... You are the only way.

Diane Ranker Riesen

His Gift

The Child is here ~ with Heaven's breath;
to save us all from sin-filled death.
What glorious news...our King is here ~
the tiny babe that conquers fear!

His birth should brighten every day....
as we have hope now~~~ in our way -
and know that heaven awaits for us,
through Jesus' blood and promised trust.

Tonight, I lay in slumber sweet ~
and know my fate is now complete...
for through our love and faithful joy -
We've been secured by this small boy!

Diane Ranker Riesen

His Snowflakes

No two snowflakes are the same ~~ each drifting towards the ground....
a huge array of frozen stars that fall without a sound -
Such mesmerizing glory that falls softly from the skies ~~~
I stand in awe while watching them come down before my eyes.

Their delicate design of perfect patterns all their own.....
Each falling from the heavens to the ground where they are blown.
I love to stand amongst them, ... their cool beauty wets my skin ~
I can't describe how sweet they are ~~ where would I begin?

It's hard to even fathom that no two have been the same ~
but then, I guess it's simple when you think of where they came.
God's works of art are marvelous ... the King of all we see.....
I cherish all the glories He creates for you and me!

Diane Ranker Riesen

His Timing

There's always a new day ~ your prayers will soon be heard...
God hears your every question and cares for every word -
He's waiting for the perfect time to answer every prayer...
just wait in silent confidence ~ for God is always there.

Time seems like forever... when the pain just seems to stay -
but God knows how to answer you in His Almighty Way.
Just hold on to His promises ~ His answer will be clear...
He hates to see you hurting and He cares for every tear.

Diane Ranker Riesen

Holy Love

To stand upon such hallowed ground ~
to sense God's breath stir all around....
with glorious trees throughout the years;
each grown toward Heaven, by God's tears.

What perfect peace surrounds my soul;
a love that mends my pieces "whole" ~~~
Miraculous views that fill the skies -
and sing out Heaven's joyful cries.

With each one blessed through unearned 'grace' -
to feel 'God's Love' surround this place.
No notes can play ~ nor words can write....
of every 'blessing' on this site.

A respite from our sin-filled world ....
a sacred jewel ~ a perfect pearl -
Upon this land my spirit soars ~~~
and leaves me deeply thirsting more!

Come join us all in sweet release.....
to feel this sanctuary's peace.
Our God is always closely near ~
He's blessed this land... He's always here!

Diane Ranker Riesen

HOME

TIFFIN, OHIO

Kindness shown .. is kindness kept ~ it's stored within your heart -
finding the people who nurture your soul… is a very good place to start.
I was born in a town that may seem slightly small - but the people are honest and true ~
the familiar faces I see on the streets.. are what brought me right back to 'YOU'.

I've lived in big cities… with so much to do ~ and I've seen what they have to show……..
but the years that I lived away from 'my home', gave me all the truths that I know.
Each one of us has the right place meant for us ~ and it's different for everyone ~
at the end of the day…. when your soul feels 'full' - you know that your search is done.

Find a place that covers your heart with love ~ where the people support you and care…..
and when you've felt this kind of peace…. You'll know you belong right there!
My hometown of Tiffin is just what I need ~ the sense of sweet peace can be felt -
My neighbors and friends shine a light on my day, and make my anxieties melt.

Your Home is not a building ~ it's not one single place….
Your 'home' brings contentment and happiness ~ a tender smile to your face.
A great home consists of a town that is filled - with hundreds of people who care ~
and once your heart feels.. all the joy that it brings…. YOU KNOW that your home is there!!

Diane Ranker Rieson

Hovering Wings

Come, sweet angels ~~ hover close;
bring me what I need the most…
let me feel some Heavenly Touch -
for it's God I need so much.

In this night - I long to sleep ~~
with God's love that I can keep.
In those hours of soft release….
may I rest in perfect peace.

And shall my prayers be clearly heard ~~
as God answers every word.
Oh, sweet assurance, then I'll feel….
for with my faith… I know You're Real.

Diane Ranker Riesen

I Believe

I ask, for now, a simple wish ~ I know You'll understand…..
the sorrows going on in this world are covering our lands.
I'm just one simple person, yet I know You hear my prayers ~
We need Your Mighty Power, Lord ~ to help things everywhere!

I know the very best for me.. Is to hand each fear to You ~
and You will answer every prayer the way You're meant to do.
I need to release every scare; and know Your Power is real….
then let my body take a rest; and soften what I feel.

For no one stands above You ~ You're the only answer true…
so I can rest much easier when I give my thoughts to You.
Thank you, Lord, for powers known ~ Your wisdom will relieve ~
each worry that confuses me… I'm grateful 'I BELIEVE'!!

Diane Ranker Riesen

I Choose

I choose to keep my 'faith' secure when everything seems wrong ~
when prayers just don't seem answered and I can't seem to feel strong.
I choose to trust God's judgement ~ and the way He answers 'prayer'....
for He's the One who knows our fates; and answers us with care.

I choose to keep believing even when I feel so lost...
and hold onto God's promises; and trust at any cost.
My prayers aren't always answered in the way I prayed they would ~
but God foresees the universe; and answers as He should.

I believe God knows what's best for me ~ although I question 'why?' ~
My human heart still breaks in two when people hurt and die.
I will not let my weakness win... God's promises are true....
and though I may not understand ~ My faith will get me through.

I choose to give my life to God... and trust His answered prayers ~
His knowledge reigns in heaven ~ and I'll see when I get there.
"Dear God forgive my anger; and my weakness when I'm torn....
You've always known what's best for me - the second I was born".

Diane Ranker Riesen

I Knew You

As soon as I laid eyes on you ~ my soul told me I knew.....
although we'd never met before... I felt that I knew you.
I know on earth it cannot be - but God's ways are not shown ~
perhaps before we came to earth.. God let our souls be known.

There's just a strange connection... like we were always friends ~
the feeling is so natural; and nothing you pretend -
There is no time in Heaven ~ and there's so much we don't know.....
who knows what God allows there.. who knows what He can show.

Your friendship makes me comfortable - your words so calm my heart....
it seems as though we never had to meet to have a 'start'.
It's so unique to find someone you've always seemed to know ~
I think we met in Heaven, then God joined us back 'below'.

Oh, what grand reunions when we all meet back above ~~~~
to see and cherish all the ones that we have ever loved!
My mind cannot imagine - the joy that will be found.....
when earthly ties no longer hold - and Heaven's gifts abound.

Diane Ranker Riesen

I Met a Man

I woke up late this morning.. with no special plans in view ~
but later on I met a man ~~ a man I never knew.
Our meeting was arranged by God - and soon I could tell why.....
he spoke about his journeys; he made me laugh and cry.

His truths were mesmerizing ~ as he told me of his life...
and witnessed his strong 'faith' in God, and how he got through strife.
I knew as soon as he was gone... I'd remember all he said ~
his simple testimony clearly showed that 'God's not dead!'.

Why do we keep our 'faith' so quiet ~ stored safely in our souls....
when we should shout it out with joy... so other people know!
I saw God's gentle spirit speaking through the words he told ~
we all need to be louder ... shout our glories, and be bold!

When all the earth is over ~ and our lives are then reviewed...
all that really matters is the witnessing we knew.
Our busy lives just seem to cause our purpose to be hid ~
but God will only care about the goodness that we did.

Don't be afraid to shout His name.... don't be too shy to say ~
that Christ, our Lord reigns in our hearts ~ and He controls our day.
How wonderful to see such faith so openly expressed....
Eternity will be your home - your faith has passed each test.

If I can reach just someone ~ and express my faith out loud...
I pray that God will lead me... on bended knees and bowed.
I met this man, today you see - who honored God with praise ~
and all the words will help me through... until I die and 'raise'!

Diane Ranker Riesen

I Never Knew

Don't cry because I am not there ~~ don't shed so many tears…
remember all the times we shared and cherish every year.
I never truly understood what 'blessings' Heaven holds…
I can't believe the beauty ~ it's far more than I was told!

Don't fear that I have left you… I am closer than before ~
I knew that things were perfect when I entered Heaven's door.
I'm with you now each moment … I'm right beside of you ~
God lets me guard you closely and enjoy the things you do.

I wish that I could prove to you each wonder that I see….
I've never been so filled with joy …. I've never felt so free!
Live out the years God planned for you - He knows what's truly best…
My soul's been with you through the years ~~ I'll be there for the rest!

Then in our sweet God's timing… you'll return yourself and 'feel'…..
till then just trust what I have said ~~~
'Yes, Heaven's really real'!!!

Diane Ranker Riesen

I Saw God

I woke up and saw God today ~~~ He's everywhere I looked…..
each view outside my window - 'How His mighty power shook'!
And I could feel His majesty displayed in every sight -
from the early morning beauty —- and the warm, soft morning light.

How glorious His power reigns ~ my soul is blessed so 'deep'..
Some days are just so beautiful… I never want to sleep.
Join me on this joyous day —- His miracles abound ~
just look for Him~ and 'feel' Him…… in every sight and sound.

Refresh yourself in all His love ~ what overwhelming bliss….
wrap yourself in all His warmth, and feel each 'Heaven's Kiss'.
Thank you, God… you've filled me ~ with such love to start my day ~
I'm anxious for the beauties that You'll show me - on my way!

Diane Ranker Riesen

I'm Going to Heaven

I know I'm going to Heaven; and I know that may sound strong;
but I've learned there is no question now and know I am not wrong.
It isn't that I've prayed so much, or hoped in earnest plea…..
but that my Christ has paid the price ~ and took my sins for me.

When you form a special bond with God….
and ask Him in your heart ~
your soul will be renewed in love;
and so much change will start.

You'll WANT to make Him proud of you ~
no work will be a chore.
For when you're pleasing God above ~
you'll want to do some more!

I often thought I'd have to earn… a special gift to go ~
but all those things were wrong I see, and now ~ I really know.
None of us could ever earn a place beside the King…..
so.. Jesus paid the price for us and conquered everything.

What glory for my soul to know ~ to never have a doubt…..
the peace I feel deep in my heart I'll never live without!
Spread the news to everyone; and let it sink down in ~~~
Yes, I'm going to Heaven! —— It's all because of Him!

Diane Ranker Riesen

Infant Love

How perfect can a newborn be ~ so perfect, pure, and whole…
who steals our hearts in seconds; and holds our very soul.
To see their tiny fingers; and their sweet and tender toes ~
brings much more magic to your life than you could ever know.

I gaze upon this infant's eyes; and marvel as he sleeps ~
I never knew a love like this could ever grow so deep.
I thought I knew what love was ~ I thought I understood….
yet not until I saw my child ~ I knew I never could.

I've never felt such holy love that asks for nothing due…
Regardless of what life will bring ~ my heart beats just for you.
Thank you, God ~ I never knew…. this blessing You would send ~
Until my eyes laid sight on him ~ I used to just pretend.

A mother's love can change the world ~ her love is just THAT strong….
and when I hold my infant child… nothing else seems wrong.
Only God could do this ~ beyond our wildest dreams ….
and I will praise You daily .. as my perfect baby beams.

A gift beyond expression.. A love that can't compare….
to any other feeling that a mother's heart can share.
Dear Lord, I'll love this baby ~ and remember every night…..
the way my soul leaped joyfully as I first saw the sight.

Diane Ranker Riesen

Jealousy

"My children, My children - why do you care what others own?
Why do you let it tease you ~ when your soul knows what it's shown?
So many gifts are given ~~ there are plenty for you all;
Each was born for certain things - and for a special cause.

From where I sit... I shake My head ......
if only you'd be glad instead —-
all those riches you desire ~
are not on earth —- they're so much 'higher'.

It's easy to get jealous when you feel so overlooked.....
but My Son lived in such angry years ~
and STILL Your sins He took!

ENVY is the opposite - of every wish I own;
Be patient, I have much for all ~~~
in time it will be known.

Please pray for others, and their dreams ~~
it only helps YOU more....
this 'joy' will feed your soul with strength -
and only bring you more!

Jealousy is useless ~ it gets you to a place....
where all MY gifts elude you, and covers up My Grace.
When you feel joy for others ~ and you're glad for what they have ~
you'll feel My blessings come to you... just as a 'healing salve'."

Diane Ranker Riesen

Judgement

As I sat in softened silence... I heard God in my soul ~
He made me understand something I really need to know....
So many times I've judged someone, and often, very strong -
but God wanted to remind me that this judgement's very wrong!

The way God made my heart feel... just brought me to my knees;
I could feel the hurt and sorrow from the people I had teased.
The ache was so intolerable ~ that I began to cry......
God wanted me to see my faults; and then He told me why.

"It's not your place to judge the acts of people here on earth -
it's not your right to place a price on what their lives are worth.
My child, you do it often ~ and you just don't realize....
I need you so to understand — I need you to know why.

There is no one but I, alone... who knows somebody's thoughts -
Prejudice is everywhere ~ and much of it was taught.
But only I can see a soul - and judge what they may do ~~~
for just like them and all who live... YOU are a sinner, too.

I ask of you compassion and a heart of empathy....
for only I can judge someone.. that job is just for ME.
Slander is so bitter ~ and I'm asking for your love ~
abide in peace with everyone.. and give to Me above.

I've always known my children would daily carry 'sin'...
it's a strong and mighty battle that none of you will win -
Show love and mercy always, and be silent of the rest ~
I, alone, will be the judge —— you just spread happiness."

Diane Ranker Riesen

I felt such peace I'd never known.. just knowing I am free -
no one's life is mine to judge ~ and I can just be 'me'!
I'm just the same as everyone, and I will always sin ~
so I am free of judging... I can leave it up to 'HIM'!!!

Diane Ranker Riesen

Just A Day

Nothing real unusual appeared throughout my day ~
but I was really blessed by God in subtle, simple ways.
I walked out into sunshine… and the warmth was everywhere….
and then I sat down on a bench and saw a cardinal there.

This bird just sat and looked at me… then it began to sing ~
I reached out very slowly, and it let me touch it's 'wing'!
I took it as a special gift…. that God sent right to me -
and as I looked around some more - there were countless things to see.

I watched three tiny bunnies rushing back into their nest…
They ventured out to see the world — then went back for a rest.
Oh, what a tender feeling …. to see those precious sights;
such sweet and gentle bunnies… and a cardinal high in flight.

It only takes some quiet time ~ to settle down your soul…..
and notice all the beauty that God's reaching out to show.
Tomorrow there'll be such views - I can't wait to see some more ~
remind yourself each morning.. that God has so much in 'store'!

Diane Ranker Riesen

Killing Babies

I sit in frozen sorrow ~ with a deeply broken heart.
What has happened to this world of ours - when did the evil start?
Time can change priorities, and minds become confused ~
Evil thoughts squeeze out the good - and logic is abused.

I don't know how to write this ~~ I have no words to show the pain…
I pray the world gets kinder, but it just gets worse again!
This time I cannot hold my voice ~ this time my voice must cry.....
How can we comprehend the fact that we let babies die!!!!

An unborn infant dwells — under another woman's heart ……
but it has its OWN body - very separate and apart.
I ache to think of all the death ~ the murder of these souls ~
and year by year these murders seem to be allowed and grow!

We have no right to bring a precious infant to its death ——
We have no right to steal this tiny angel's life and breath.
Knowing of the love of God, with His children made so pure ~
HOW can anyone explain the torture they endure!

This time I can't stay quiet ~ and I'll scream until you hear…
that killing unborn babies has brought 'HELL' so very near.
These babies will be Heaven-Bound, and need no human prayer ~
but, those of 'man' who murder them - this pain I cannot bear.

Sweet angels fly up to your home — heaven waits for your return.
My soul pleads prayers that one day all the people here will learn….
We have NO RIGHT to end a life that God's ordained to live ~
I'll pray in earnest hope that God will hopefully 'forgive'.

Diane Ranker Riesen

Legacy

My legacy lies not in all the accolades I've won ~
nor does it lie in all the different things that I have done.
It lies in how I held so tightly to my Father's hand…
when things in life just didn't go the way that I had planned.

When I meet my God face to face; and look into His eyes…
the one thing that will matter, "Did I trust Him through my 'why's?"
God doesn't look at all my things; and hard work that I've done ~
He looks at how I lived for Him, in His name… through His Son.

It lies in how I loved Him even through my hardest pain….
and lies in how I thanked Him — when nothing was to gain.
It doesn't matter what I own, or places I have been ~
it only matters how I kept my love and faith in Him.

God wants us to enjoy our lives; He wants us to embrace…
all the gifts He's given us ~ enjoying every place.
But most of all, our lives are meant to share our faith with man ~
and when He knows we've finished… He'll take us home again!

Diane Ranker Riesen

Life

Whenever I think of the blessings I've seen ~
the truths I've discovered, the lessons I've gleaned …
I'm always amazed at this thing we call "life";
and the strength each soul has during difficult strife.

No matter the hardship, the trials and the pain -
It seems we all get up and stand tall again ~
though the sorrows remain, and the scars slowly heal….
we keep our compassion and struggle to 'feel'.

Bend down to the lonely man sitting outside ~
or reach out to anyone crying inside.
The love that is given comes back largely grown…
and gives you a feeling like you've never known.

For TRUE happiness isn't found standing clear…
it's not always simple ~ or lingering near ~
but you find it whenever your heart sheds some care….
and in time you will learn that it lives EVERYWHERE!

That lady you smiled at… was feeling so down…
you created a smile ~ and got rid of her frown.
You showed her that LOVE still abides strong and tall ~
and this, my dear friend - is far greater than all!

Diane Ranker Riesen

Like Yesterday

My loved one passed so long ago ~
and though much time has passed…
Sometimes, it seems like yesterday -
when I saw you the last.

At first I thought my life was gone ~
and nothing helped my heart….
I've learned to keep your love with me -
since we were torn apart.

The "grief", it never goes away ~
I knew it never would…..
But as each new day passes by;
I've done the best I could.

I want to make you proud of me ~
to show you I am strong….
but some days just don't show it -
and everything seems wrong.

I'll keep on trying best I can ~
I know you hate my pain…..
and so I'll use the love you gave….
until we're back again.

Diane Ranker Riesen

Lost Loved Ones

I have some special loved ones.. who help me every day ~
but certain times throughout the year ~ they need to heal my way.
I miss them every hour of time; but there are always weeks....
when I need more attention- and I long for them to speak.

They left this earth in different ways - and each one broke my heart;
I never could imagine living here with them apart.
I've felt such grief, and know the pain ~ I want it like before.....
but through these journeys in the dark..God's taught me so much more.

I'd never say we should not grieve.... our hearts aren't meant to break ~
I'd never say to understand; there's truths our minds can't take;
but through my trials and heartache ~ I've learned beyond the pain...
that there's a place we all will join... and see them once again.

I believe that God's Great Power can change the hardest heart..
and I believe that death can't keep our loved ones far apart.
Our earthly bodies wither; and will never remain 'whole' ~
but God made us eternal ~ and will never harm our 'soul'.

My special ones are always near ~ and though I cannot 'see' ~
I've learned God lets their real selves live, and linger close to me.
Fresh grief is overwhelming.... it can tear our life apart ~
but somehow all our special souls ~ will help our hurting heart.

Our earthly body's temporary ~ it only lasts while 'here'....
but then when we reach Heaven... we will understand so 'clear';
that worldly deaths are just a stop ~ when we miss loved ones here ~
but I believe God lets their souls move freely; and stay near.

It still will hurt so many times ~ grief doesn't melt away....
but we can hold their memories ~ don't let the anger stay.
Eternity is longer ~ earthly time is very small ~~~
hold firmly to your Faith in God until we're with them all.

Diane Ranker Riesen

Love Wins

I pray that morning brings some peace; and calms our worried hearts…
We all have troubles hovering near….. with power to pull apart -
I seem to just enjoy the normal good things that occur…
but notice, oh so quickly … when there's hurt that I endure.

I have such countless reasons to be thankful every day ~
but tend to overlook them all ~ when pain enters my way.
I minimize the joyful gifts and maximize the trials….
it seems so wrong to live that way ~ God's with me all the while.

Lord, work on me throughout this night, to change my point of view;
teach my soul to intercede ~ and change the things I do.
Each problem takes my strength away; although You are so near.
Teach my heart to reach for You when sorrows linger here.

We can't change each trial that comes ~ but we can choose our ways;
And I pray You show me through this night —- to cherish every day.
Some days are so much harder; and I let them steal the "power" -
that You give me so freely ~~ to handle every hour.

'Happiness, sweet joy, and love' are stronger through and through ~
and I can counteract my fears when I keep my eyes on 'You'.
Now I lay me down to sleep surrendering my fears…
and trust to feel Your presence even closer…… always 'here'.

Diane Ranker Riesen

Magic Carpet

I'm on a magic carpet ride ~ oh, how I long to see-
all the wonders of this world, and God's divinity.
Glide me past the mountains, so stately as they stand…
and let me notice all the power that lies within God's hand.

Through the meadows, I will glide… and smell the countless flowers ~
what joy I'll feel and peace I'll have..as I ride through the hours.
Perhaps I'll find a rainbow ~ and slide down to the end…
and when I'm done, I'll simply ask… and ride it once again!

Fly me over the oceans, and let me watch the tides….
the waves contain such beauty; and such 'life' the waters hide.
The seagulls soar around me… with their soft and flowing wings ~
and I stare closely at their flights ~ as all of nature sings.

Just as my ride is ending… I'll glide up through the clouds ~
my soul will leap with happiness ~ my tears will cry out loud.
Our God has given all of us - a world too great to know—-
take some time to notice it… sit back; enjoy the show!

Diane Ranker Riesen

Mary's Birth

"My sweet, dear child ~ Your time is near…
I'm so ashamed and filled with fear.
I feel You stir below my heart ~~~
and know Your birth will quickly start.

For who am I ~ this lowly one —-
that God ordained to have His Son?
Just simple, and so barely known ~
for God to choose me from His Throne!

I pray to You… my unborn Son ~
to give me strength as birth's begun.
I have no worldly gifts to share…
and just a straw-filled place waits there.

This shelter built ~~ not for a King..
no warmth but soon…. the Angels sing!!
While through my pain ~ I wait to see….
the Mighty Son of God through me.

My precious Child… my Babe for now ~
will die to save the world somehow.
But - please for now … just be my 'Son'-
before Your worldly works begun."

Diane Ranker Riesen

Mighty as a Tree

Oh, how I wish my 'faith' could be ~~ as strong and mighty as a tree…
a faith that will not bend or sway ~ and strengthens right along with me.
I want to grow deep roots with it, and firmly stand my ground ~~~~
whenever trials come my way, or any test is found.

I stand amazed at all the force a normal tree can bear…..
amid such giant gusts of wind…. it still is standing there.
That's how I want my Faith to be ~ and I pray every day….
that God will send His Mighty Power and strengthen me that way.

Just like a tree needs nourishment… I'll keep my prayer life strong ~
and with each hour my soul will grow, and be where it belongs.
The glorious proof and Strength of God - is shown in every tree ——
Imagine all the perfect Power that God can put in ME!

Diane Ranker Riesen

Miraculous

In all the earth ~~~ no sweeter sound -
than when a soft "heartbeat" is found.
God blessed another soul to 'breathe'.....
no greater wonder…. to believe.

What miracles our Master holds —
each glorious infant to behold…
and I shall never understand ~~~
the power God holds within His hands.

Much thankfulness, in me, abides —-
when each new infant starts to cry.
Each child, so wondrous and unique ~~~
such songs of praise…. I cannot speak!

Diane Ranker Riesen

Morning Dance

Take a morning dance with me ~
let's dream the dreams we hope will 'be'.
The music of our universe is just outside our door -
let's listen to the melodies and dance.. then dance some more!

The lullabies play through the trees ~
sweet songs are humming in the breeze....
let's take the time to just be free ————-
enjoying every sight we see.

Oh, the warmth that wraps me tight ...
from every ray of soft sunlight -
We need to always take the time ~
and notice all of nature's rhyme.

We'll dance among the flowers.. and leap among the leaves ~
We'll look around and notice all the joys that we believe!
What beauty lies within our world ~ and dreams wait to come true....
I'll wait for you to get here.... and dance away with you!

Diane Ranker Riesen

Morning Lilies

Morning Lilies stretch their arms and reach up toward the sun ~~
within the hour, all sorted flowers have yawned until they're done.
Then spread out like a blanket - lies the rainbow covered ground....
and I am stunned at all the perfect beauty I have found.

Butterflies begin to wake; and dance amongst the leaves -
while hummingbirds begin to sing of all my heart believes.
I marvel at this majesty ... as I stand still and gaze ~~
at all the beauty God has formed ~ I stand in awe .. amazed.

With all the gorgeous paintings God has formed throughout our land;
and all the colors blended into 'visions' as I stand ~
I find it quite amazing to imagine what I've missed....
every tiny beauty God has formed ~ the glories that He's kissed.

How wondrous and how precious that I have the chance to see....
all creations formed by God that wait so quietly for me.
Each day I seem to notice something different and brand new ~
and anxiously await another wonder in my view!

Diane Ranker Riesen

Morning Peace

Good morning Sunshine ~ hello Breeze…..
welcome bunnies, flowers, and trees.
My eyes wake up to wondrous sights ~
my heart is full… my soul feels right.

I've learned that life flies by so fast….
each year seems shorter than the last.
I realize now that each day shines ~~
and it's a gift to enjoy mine.

There's nothing 'hatred' can repair ~
and sorrow only strips you bare…..
and so, this morning - Lord, I pray =
My 'faith' in You will guide my way.

You've given me this day to be……
a version of the best of 'me'!
I pray that all Your peace will stay ~
with EVERYONE throughout this day.

Diane Ranker Riesen

My Promise

I'll say the same thing this year ~ like every year before…
to be a kinder person… and offer help to more.
But I fall short and weeks fly by - and my resolutions fade -
I need to place this promise deep inside me and obey.

There are so many people who could use a helping hand ~
So many needs outnumbered by the pains they all have made.
Everything seems busier ~ and hours disappear…
But there's really one main reason… why all of us are here.

Smile at all the people who cross your path today…
Find someone who looks all alone; and say 'hello' someway.
It can be hard to reach out to a friend you haven't seen ~
But there's such magic being 'nice' and helping someone's dream.

If I decide to really change ~ I can't rely on "me"….
I need to give this choice to God so He can help it be.
Once I start this venture; and I see the joy it brings ~~~
I know a sense of happiness will shower everything.

There isn't much that's left to life ~ when all your days are through…
It's not about the things you have… but, all the things you do.
"Lord, help me to remember and remind me when I fall;
And then I'll know my life had purpose; and I had lived it all!"

Diane Ranker Riesen

My Special Time

There is a 'joy' not far away ~
it happens every time I pray.
My heartbeat slows to quiet peace....
my soul blooms large, and worries cease.

This quiet time can't be compared...
to any other time that's shared.
Magic looms and fills the air;
a Holy love is everywhere.

This special time is anywhere....
when I slow down enough for 'prayer'.
How great a gift we each own 'free'...
God's always waiting there for me!

Diane Ranker Riesen

My Truth is Real

Sometimes I just imagine that you're sitting next to me ~~
your death had never happened and it's how it used to be...
but in due time I realize that everything is true -
I never thought that I would have to manage without you.

I couldn't wait to wake each morn and spend my hours with you....
but now I wake and you're not here ~~~ I don't know what to do -
They say that it gets easier - they say time helps the pain .....
but I would give up everything - to have you back again.

The sun comes up each morning, and then moonlight fills the skies ~~
the world just keeps on turning... as I struggle and I try -
somehow I make it through each day ... but sorrow fills the air...
while everyone is smiling ―― to me it isn't fair.

Yet somewhere deep inside of me ~ a strength comes merging through....
a very special sense of hope that helps me without you ~
this tender power rises up - just when I feel so weak ―――
my spirit tells me God is here... my soul can feel Him speak.

"Hold on dear child, I'll carry you through every darkened day ~
and though your pain is still so real... I'll help you find your way...
consequences fill My world with pain that's hard to bear -
But I am right here with you when each hour seems unfair.

One day My World will be renewed - and all pain will decease ~
you'll be with Me in Heaven, and you'll have such perfect peace.
The questions that torment you now ~ the loneliness you feel....
will be erased forever ~ for My child — My truths are real".

Diane Ranker Riesen

My Turn

Why am I fearful of my death .. why don't I want to 'leave'?
Each of us will have an end; and I know I 'BELIEVE'!
I guess I think I'll miss so much, and not be here to see….
but Heaven makes it perfect ~ and things will stay with me.

I love my friends and family so ~~~ and want to see their days…..
Yet I forget the Power of God… and all His Mighty Ways.
I really won't be gone at all - my spirit will stay close ~~~
and everything I want to see will stay with me the most.

I wish we all got solid PROOF - a glimpse of where we'll be…..
But Faith is what sustains me, and makes me just 'believe' ~
I asked my God to come to me - and stay within my soul ——
He's there right now, and this I know …. I'll have a place to go!

No human mind can comprehend the beauty that's ahead…
why would I want to stay right here .. and not see THAT instead?
It's just the fear of the unknown - it can play upon your fears~~~~
but what a joy to know one day… there won't be any tears!

I'll stay here as God wants me to - and cherish every day ~
but when He calls me Home to Him… I won't get in the way.
I'll see again my loved ones that have gone ahead of me…
and when your time for Heaven comes… that is where I'll be!

Diane Ranker Riesen

New Blessing

I met someone not long ago ~ someone I'd never known....
I wondered why it took so long; but I was quickly shown -
that God has perfect timing, and He has a mighty plan ~
He brings new people in your life.. exactly 'where' and 'when'.

Sometimes they're for encouragement.. and often just for fun ~
but God knows who we always need; and sends the perfect 'one'.
Often they come just in time when things seems dark and grey ~
and they come by just randomly ~ to brighten up your day!

Sometimes they come for comfort ~ when you feel so all alone....
they were the perfect answer; and God has always known.
It still amazes me at times ~ how God knows every need ~
and sends a new friend to my life… to plant a blessed 'seed'.

Don't take for granted who you meet.. don't wonder why they're there -
before you even asked Him ~ God sent 'answer to a prayer'.
Let yourself be used by Him.. when He hears someone's plea ~
I've found when I get called by Him…. it always blesses "ME"!

Diane Ranker Riesen

Night Answer

Whisk me up ~ into the night …
let me see it from 'Your' view.
Since I've always seen it from 'my' eyes,
how does it look to You?

I stood outside and waited…
then I said a little prayer -
What happened next surprised me!
God answered me right there!

"Oh child, you can't imagine ~
how I see earth from My eyes….
with all My children slowing down…
as moonbeans flutter by.

Each creature that I molded…
is settling down to rest ~
the deer and birds find places to sleep;
as babies do the best.

My view is somewhat different ~
It's really rather rare….
As I smile down upon the earth -
I see your rising 'prayers'!

Enjoy the beauty as you gaze -
each night sings out it's songs…
then let your tired mind be still;
you're right where you belong."

Diane Ranker Riesen

I won't forget that special night ~
When God heard my small plea...
Nighttime holds more meaning now....
and God's right here with me.

Diane Ranker Riesen

Night Praise

I think tonight I'll close my eyes, say my prayers, and go to bed ~
Today was such a blessing and I heard the words God said.
He spoke to me through every brush of sweet air past my face;
and showed me His great Majesty, around me, EVERYPLACE !

The birds sang me a lullaby; as I strolled down the street....
and every time I took a turn ~ I found another treat.
God's love lives all around us... in each flower, bush, and tree ~
and because of this... I know that God is always close to me.

Thank you for another day ~ and now I'll take my rest....
tomorrow will be more surprises. O' how I will be blessed!
I pray Your angels cover over every one tonight ~~~
Your Power supersedes all hurt, and makes the world feel right.

Diane Ranker Riesen

Night Wonders

Up upon your tired wings ~ take me to the nightly moon…..
May I vision all of nature settling down in perfect tune.
Oh, the night.. can be so quiet ~ and the darkness stills the air…
but in soft and sweet surrender- you will feel God waiting there.

As the tree leaves curl for slumber, and the birds still down to rest ~
Sometimes in this perfect quiet… I can hear my God the best.
His Majesty too large to fathom… earth spins slowly in the air ~
as God commands each timely moment - all His Power is showing there.

I cry in awe of all the beauty… every gift our God has made ~
all His creatures nestle down; and all His children softly laid.
Who can do such marvelled wonders? Only God can rule the sky….
now take me down upon your feathers - let me feel the breeze move by.

Diane Ranker Riesen

No End

My eyes can see you everywhere ~
my ears can hear your voice....
I feel you in the quiet times -
and even in the noise.

I see you in the nighttime ...
and I hear you in each song;
if I just take a moment ~
I can tell you're never gone.

You twinkle in the stars at night...
and touch me with the rain ~
God gives me such security -
I'll see you once again.

Our souls are so much stronger...
than the bodies we live in.
The end of earthly limits is
a new chance to begin!

Each time I'm feeling lonely...
I can simply close my eyes ~~
and feel your spirit next to me -
for no one really dies.

Diane Ranker Riesen

No GOD?

Galaxies and galaxies within our universe ~
with every star aligned just right... and from a 'cosmic burst????'
Each moon turns perfectly in tune; rotating as it should~
with every cell and molecule creating unique good.

I find it very hard to think that there's no Higher Power ~
Who supervised creation without a time or hour.
Can anyone explain to me how all this came to be?
The seasons working perfectly; and all that we can see?

Who can make a single blade of grass and make it grow....
who can light the stars up high and make such perfect glow?
I look at all the majesty that shines upon our earth ~
and can't believe there is No Power — far beyond our worth.

If someone could explain it ~~~ all the miracles that 'show'.....
I think we'd have it figured out; and would already 'know'.
But most of all, it shows we have a Mighty Power above ~~
and we should work each day to show Him all our thanks and love.

Without Him there'd be nothing ~ and you would not exist;
but here you are, right here and now ~~~ how could you resist.....
the fact that God is Sovereign and has governed all the skies;
just trust your feelings deep inside and stop your questions, 'Why'?

Diane Ranker Riesen

No One Else

There is no one who can compare ~
to Christ, My Lord - who's always there.
All things just pale compared to Him…
all earthly help grows deeply dim.

When I am hurting, tired, or sad….
when everything appears so bad ~
I close my eyes, and say a prayer….
and without fail, God's always there.

Release your trials and rest your mind -
It's in His hands; much peace you'll find.
Our God stands near us, always 'here'….
to calm each fear; and dry each tear.

How great to know we have Him close ~
how perfect that God always knows…..
We need not fight our trials alone;
let God make all your hurts His Own!

> Diane Ranker Riesen

Offer up Your Worries

We have a choice each morning; and often, I choose wrong ~
I choose to do things by myself; and forget the 'One' who's strong.
I wake up in an anxious mood and decide to fight the day....
when all along I forget to lean on God; and start to pray.

Sometimes things seem so helpless; and a purpose can't be found ~
I try to do things on my own; and ignore the help around.
I need to just remember~~ that before I'm out of bed....
to close my eyes and pray to God - and use His strength instead.

I tell myself this often — then I always slip away ~~
I need to promise, heart and soul .... to do this Every day.
On those days I still don't seem to feel the change I need;
God knows just what the future holds; and guides me to succeed.

Don't ever feel you have to carry all your pains alone ~
There's just a greater Power that has always seen and known...
just hand your worries up to Him; and never take them back;
God knows the troubles hurting you ~ He'll give you what you lack.

Diane Ranker Riesen

Oh, Heaven

Cold and brisk upon my cheek ~ God's breath is all around—-
as Winter blows its mighty power; and falls on to the ground.
So white and pure - each flake unique; as I gaze on the sight...
what wondrous beauty God shares freely...on this Winter night.

I often wonder silently.. when I see these perfect views ~
of sparkling glitter on the land with tints of opal hues.....
how Heaven must be waiting ~ to show us all God made;
and just how quickly all these sights will surely start to fade.

For God has saved the best for last ~ with scenes compared to none;
I wait, in earnest patience .... to see all that He's done!
The colors will be different ~ as I've never seen before...
and I will fall in reverent awe when I see Heaven's door.

Yet, still while I await that time... God gives me much to see ~
from every perfect snowflake and every white tipped tree.
Not even in my dreams at night .. can I ponder His pure home....
Yet know one day, I'll be with Him ~ and call His place 'my own'.

Diane Ranker Riesen

Oh, Night!

Oh, how close my God's to me ~
when I look closely at a tree.
And when the night's moon casts its glow …
God's perfect love is there, I know.

What powers beam throughout the skies..
as breezes blow, and night birds fly.
I sense His presence in the air ~
and feel His magic everywhere!

Such glorious gifts God shows at night ~
within each star's amazing sight….
I stand amazed at every view;
I feel such peace ~ and you will, too.

Don't just enjoy God's daylit hours…
with rays of warmth and precious flowers—-
remember, night time brings sweet dreams ~
beneath His golden, moonlit beams.

Diane Ranker Riesen

Oh, Sweet Babies

Oh, sweet babies… night draws near ~ with moonlight shining down….
the time has come for slumber; and for peace to settle 'round.
Such magic softness fills your souls - and gives you grace for sleep ~
May Our Great God in Heaven hold you in His arms to keep.

I pray your dreams be magical - and filled with gentle love…
as you hear angels lullabies sing softly from above.
Be still, sweet babies ~ gently rest.. until the morning dawns ~
and then, in tender starting light…. stretch wide and softly yawn.

A brand new day is surfacing; and you have much to learn…
and then, in time you all will lay your 'own babes' down, in turn ~
Cherish every touch of love, and build a soul of "joy"..
let night time slumber bless you all….. God touch each girl and boy.

Diane Ranker Riesen

Once Again

So many years since we've been close ~
I miss your face, and hugs the most.
Yet I have memories stored down deep -
and they resurface when I sleep.

I know you're really never gone…
our souls will see no end ~
but there are times I want you here.
Sometimes, I just pretend.

I imagine that you're at the door;
and walk in with that smile.
I pretend to spend the day with you ~
and push away 'denial'.

But truthfully, I am not wrong ~
your spirit's always here.
It's different than it used to be,
but still I know you're near.

One day, all pretense will be gone;
I'll see you, in the whole ~
and then I'll get to relive all
that's stored within my soul.

Diane Ranker Riesen

Our Angel

There are times when God decides to make a special dream come true ~
He saw our love and answered us… and that's when He made 'You'.
Perfection pure as Heaven - with starlight in your eyes…..
We cherished every moment, every smile ~ and every cry.

To hold you was a blessing… one we never will forget ~
and though our hearts are breaking, your life holds no regret…..
for you, our precious angel - is worth each scar and tear -
You gave us everything we need ~ and more, within one year.

Sometimes God allows our pain, although He's hurting, too ~
but YOU were very special, and God really needed you.
The Heavens are much brighter now… the angels sing in praise-
and we will ever love and honor all your earthly days.

We'll love you every second, and we know you're in such peace.
When God decides the time is right - we, too will be released.
And then together for all time ~ we'll hold you once again ~
Fly high, our precious Angel ~ be joyful until then!

Diane Ranker Riesen

Our Christ

From humble birth... to painful death ~
nothing more than all the rest;
the Christ child infant, free of sin...
and born to bring us 'Life' again.

He walked along the dusty paths...
and suffered such horrendous wrath ~
and though He could have stopped it all-
Christ Jesus stayed true to His call.

For thirty years, He walked the crowds ~
and spoke so boldly... clear and loud;
that He was born God's mighty Son...
and tried to teach what should be done.

Though many followed Him in peace...
His haters taunts would never cease.
In spite of all the anger shown ~
He stayed to preach God's word alone.

The ending was as He began ~~
a humble life; to live God's plan.
His words were filled with love and peace,
and showed the way for sin's release.

His death was 'torture' on a tree ~
but He remained for you and me.
He proved His Majesty in the end...
when He arose from death, Amen.

Diane Ranker Riesen

Our Country

There can be no great peace within this "land built under God"...
when no one can agree on how to live these grounds we trod.
My heart aches at the thought of how God's trust has been ignored ~
I wonder if you don't believe ~ then what are you 'here' for?

This mighty nation is a gift of far, unreaching pride.....
but lately, something's missing - many things have seemed to die.
Disagreements cover all our land ~ and compromise seems lost -
it seems to me we'd want to save God's love at any cost.

No one's ever always 'wrong' ~~ and no one's always 'right' ....
It takes great strength to compromise, and courage not to 'fight'.
Being built 'under our God' makes certain rules secure ~
although we may not love each rule, by 'faith' we MUST endure.

I pray for our great Country ~ and I pray for all of 'Man'......
I pray the tides will turn, and everyone will understand ~
that compromise and peace can be created if we try-
and if not soon - I fear our land of freedom soon will die.

Diane Ranker Riesen

Our Fight for God

They'll always be some people who will strangely look your way ~
and whisper of the words you write and things you want to say;
but Faith in God is worth it ~ and God sees your very soul....
He watches from the Heavens, and He will prove it so.

When you show other people of the love you hold inside ~
and you announce your truth is true... God never let's you die.
Your earthly days are numbered; but your real life will begin....
as quickly as you close your eyes ~ You'll be right there with Him!

What awesome glory waits for those who believe that God is real...
and give their life to Him each day ~ and shout out what they feel.
For nothing in this world will ever top what joys you'll see...
when earthly life is ended and your soul is finally 'free'.

Diane Ranker Riesen

Our Gifts

No one really knows us ~ although they really try…
They think they understand us; but they'll never know our 'cry'.
Imagining the pain that comes when babies do not live ~
is something we can't show them… it's something we can't give.

A parent who has lost a child can be compared to none….
and in the end years of our life ~ the battle is not won.
We carry secret heartaches that no one else can see ~
we learn to go on living … but we're never truly free.

God chose us for some reason; and I cannot fathom 'why?'-
He gave us such a miracle ~ and then He let it die.
But our minds cannot understand why God allows such pain ~
all the constant wondering in this world.. will always be in vain.

We helped God bring a special soul; and it will always 'be';
somewhere up in Heaven ~ this 'soul' will wait for me.
We're warriors of a special kind .. who suffer unknown loss ~
we've learned to trust God's mighty will and strive at any cost.

Our babies are not gone at all ~ their souls remain so strong….
we need to wait to hold them; even though it seems so wrong.
Thank you, God, for giving us these precious souls to keep ~
and hold us closely in Your Love as silently, we weep.

One day we'll have them back with us… eternity is real ~
and when we reach that point in life; there's no pain that we'll feel.
All our babies will be there - beyond those pearly gates….
they're living in such glory; as our earthly bodies wait.

Diane Ranker Riesen

Our Mighty One

I've walked a thousand miles ~ and I've seen so many views....
I've seen the pain our world can cause; and seen what 'love' can do.
I've watched a baby struggling; with each breath to stay alive ~
and celebrated joyous thanks when that small baby thrives.

I've seen the death of many... who have fought the mighty fight ~
and sensed a change within the room when that tired person dies.
Heaven sends us moments when our hearts are nearly broke...
and I've heard silent whispers... in my ears ~ when 'angels' spoke.

My human self can be so tired... my strength can be so worn ~
but then I'm gifted somehow; by new glory that is born.
I know I'll have my worried days ~ and struggle through the night....
but just when I am weakest ~ God sends me 'hope' in sight.

Hold on, be strong and listen.... Be still and know God 'is'....
He holds our mighty universe; and all the earth is "His".
Don't ever let hate capture you ~ don't let doubts ever win ~
for just when life seems hopeless... God gives us strength again.

Diane Ranker Riesen

Our Savior Stayed

Our Savior stayed upon that cross ~
He breathed His last to pay our cost.
What sacrifice when He was pure —
to freely take what He endured.

How could He bear such misery….
while mocked and bleeding, on that tree.
This unearned gift, in pain, endured ~~~~
to give our lives a perfect cure.

Christ Jesus always had the power…
but chose to suffer through each hour.
What perfect love; ~ as never known…
He took our sins on…. as His own.

This crucifixion so intense -
with sorrows undescribed…….
Our Savior loved us endlessly,
and proved it when He died.

Diane Ranker Riesen

Our Truth

I cannot imagine a world without Faith ~ a world that will end and be done....
all of this majesty shown all around ~ in the meadows, the flowers, the sun.
Why would a place of such beauty exist ... if there wasn't a great master plan?
The thought that we die and it all goes away ~ is something I can't understand.

Intricate miracles surround us each day, each breath that we take is
a sign ~
that there's Someone much greater than any of us.. who is Mighty,
and greatly divine!
What purpose is there to a life that will end ~ and nothing
continues from there.....
my mind and my heart feel my 'soul' deep inside; and it has to continue somewhere.

This isn't a dream ~ our earth stands firm and real... and each of us really exist -
what sense would it make for the beauties we see...
and the loved ones that we'll never miss?
The Proof of our God is quite easy to see... there's a purpose for all that we do;
'Reality' proves His incredible Power and the future for me and you.

Diane Ranker Riesen

Peace

There are moonbeams just around the bend ~ as daytime hours come to end....
and all the flowers begin to fold... as willow branches start to bend.
It seems all nature knows just when — it's time to slow and time to rest....
most people seem to love the day... but I think I like night the best.

No busy, hurrying, hectic chores ~ nor people so confused —
the ending of the busy hours with so much time abused.
Night is quiet, sweet, and slow ~ I hear its lullabies......
as children settle down for sleep, and softly close their eyes.

Oh, night... I so look forward - to seeing you each day ~
my mind relaxes all its thoughts and I can clearly 'pray'.
Thank you, God, for night's sweet gifts~ the tender feel of peace....
the day brings many joyful times.. but night brings soft release.

Diane Ranker Riesen

Perfect View

From my view .. I see the stars——
sparkling diamonds where they are..
with such beauty few possess ~
a dazzling show... above the rest!

Oh, the brilliance my eyes see ~
such peaceful joy encumbers me.
I could sit and stare all night -
at this glorious, Godly sight.

Then when I retreat to sleep——
Starlight stays ~ so I can keep....
their soft and gentle glow stays near ~
I feel God's Power shown so clear.

Don't miss the magic of the skies....
the beauty forms "tears' in my eyes ~
and makes my soul so strongly yearn -
for another evening to return!

Diane Ranker Riesen

Perfectly Imperfect

What difference does it make if I am thin, or I am round?
~ and then I slipped from bed and put my knees upon the ground.....
Thank you, God, for making me the way you saw was best ~
and help me be so grateful that I'm different from the rest.

In truth, it doesn't matter what we look like from outside ~
None of that will mean a thing once we have lived and died.
The true worth of a person is how much they loved and cared....
God looks at how we honored Him; and how we gave and shared.

God formed you in His image ~ and He made you perfectly....
when earthly life is over... it's your 'soul' that will be free.
Be proud of who you really are... the 'love' that's in your soul ~
beauty is so fleeting... it's God's truths that make us whole.

Diane Ranker Riesen

Please, Lord

Oh, my heart, my heart, oh Lord ~
my soul is aching to its core…..
Loved ones hurting terribly -
send Your comfort 'there' for me.

When the time is dark as black…
ease their pain… in strong attack ~
Let them feel sweet heaven's breath -
and help their faith win over death.

Oh what glory waits so near ~
I pray in love, but - with a tear….
until they feel Your Paradise,
and see Your face before their eyes.

Diane Ranker Riesen

Quiet Snow

Fall softly, ever gently, with such silence to my ear ~
as I wait in simple joy...to see the 'whiteness' gather near.
A sparkling blanket covers...as the flakes begin to merge —-
I watch the glittering diamonds as I feel my passions surge.

Such majesty begins to gleam ~ as Heaven's beauty shows...
and such a cushioned layer of pure softness starts to grow.
I find myself immersed in glorious wonder at the sight -
of such a glistening show of God's perfection in the light.

What wonders rest beyond the bounds of earthly limits wait...
I pause in awe of what I'll see beyond our 'Heaven's Gate'.
Oh, God - our master artist, what beauties shall I see ~
I smile in anxious joy for each new gift awaiting me.

But for this while, I'll be content… to watch this wondrous snow ~
as precious jewels of sparkles dance when drifts begin to blow.
Oh, what a sight of miracles ~ a view of Our God's Hand…..
I watch the unique snowflakes flutter down across the land.

Diane Ranker Riesen

Quiet

How quiet comes the evening air ~
as Heaven's nature settles there…
in sweet surrender to the day -
time to rest has come your way.

In this eve of close embrace ~
Brings now a time to rest your pace…
and let your weary body lay -
to wash away the hectic day.

Search in all this silence…
for a tender place to rest.
Tomorrow will come soon enough ~
find shelter ~ peace is best.

And then when morning reappears..
as it has always done ~
You'll be renewed in spirit..
a new day has begun.

Diane Ranker Riesen

Real!

I want to show my 'gratefulness' on days when I am lost ~
I want to praise God everyday.. His Love is worth the cost.
I want to show the strength He gives when I am filled with pain;
and be content on days I feel my heart is full of 'rain'.

He's there for me through everything ~ and I should do the same;
I want to smile and pray to Him.. and sing His mighty name!
For God stays right here with me ~~~ no matter how I feel ~
I want to keep reminding Him— I KNOW that He is real!!!!!!!!

He stands so firmly by me, and helps me every day ~
He guides me where I need to be; and walks me on the way.
Thank you, God, for all Your love ~ I cherish all Your Powers-
and can't imagine life without You by me every hour!!!!!

Diane Ranker Riesen

Remember

Take a trip inside your mind..
you'll be surprised at what you find ~
so many memories are stored in place.....
so many thoughts that time's erased.

Sometimes they come out in your dreams....
and once again - they're real it seems.
Time can make your memory weak ~
so close your eyes and take a peek!

You'll start to notice memories.....
those stored up thoughts will be set free -
then once again you'll get to feel ~~~
past moments that will seem so real.

Quiet time will help you find ~
such wondrous memories in your mind.
Remembering days of years gone by....
assure that they will never die.

Diane Ranker Riesen

Right Beside You

Don't miss me when you're tired ~
or when you're all alone.
Don't miss me when you're older...
there's so much still unknown.

I'd rather have you smiling..
when memories come your way~
I'd rather have you cherish all the
love we shared each day.

Don't feel alone when holidays begin and I'm not there;
I have a secret for you, "I'm staying EVERYWHERE!"

I know if you could see me, for a second ~
you would know....
that I'm right where I so want to be-
within our Heaven's glow.

But that's not how it works up here~
You have to dig down deep....
and blindly trust God's promises;
I hate to see you weep.

Try hard to hold on strongly...
to the Faith I know you own ~
I'll be so proud and happy.....
I'm right here ~~~~ you're not alone.

Diane Ranker Riesen

Say My Name

We need to tell you something ~~ please listen close, my friends ….
When we have lost a precious child……. DON'T say you understand.
We 'long' to hear our children's names; it brings us so much peace ~~
they lived, and loved, and we still care - although they are deceased.

To us, our children still remain in every breath and thought ~~~
We live each day remembering the things they did and taught.
Every time you hug us ~~~ and you whisper us their name ——
You'll never know the 'blessing'; and our day won't be the same.

Although each year grows longer.. And past memories seem to fade ~
A parent never loses all the moments that were made.
The older that we get in years ~ we seem to miss them more….
our hearts will be made whole again at Heaven's Holy door.

Diane Ranker Riesen

Search

A willow bends in honor.. to the Sun who feeds its leaves ~
a heart can mend and heal ~ although it's hard to just believe.
There's so much in this world of ours- with wonders so unknown....
I tend to just ignore these gifts—- until they're really shown.

An old man sits up on his porch and bows his head in prayer ~
his pleas to God are changing things... and we don't know he's there.
How many things I miss each day ~ I know there is so much....
a broken soul is mended by a total stranger's touch.

What mystery surrounds us all.... beneath the clouds and sky ~
I seem to miss so much of it ~ and often... wonder why?
I guess 'life' just goes swiftly by and I don't stop to see......
all the wondrous beauty that surrounds and comforts me.

I vow to open up my eyes .. and search each day to see..........
all the earthly miracles that God is sending me.
A baby cries and time stands still.. until the crying ends;
 ~ as once again, within my view... another willow bends.

Diane Ranker Riesen

Security

What a glorious morning, Lord ~~~ I woke up to Your 'love';
and I can feel Your comfort... all Your help sent from above.
Even if this day seems wrong, and problems come my way ~
I know You'll be right with me... to get me through the day.

What comfort knowing You are there - such peace within my soul....
to know I always have You to guide my way and show....
what I should do when I'm afraid; or feeling very torn ~
I know You've always been with me; each day since I've been born.

And I can make it with Your help ~ no matter what life brings...
I'll pray to You and offer up each sad and troubling thing.
Thank You, Lord... for being here; I know my day's secured.
You've always rescued me from every sorrow I've endured.

What peace to know I have You... what a gift I have in You!
I believe Your word is truthful ~ and believe each thing You do.
I'll trust You even in the midst of daunting trials that come....
for I have such security in knowing.. 'You're the One'!

Diane Ranker Riesen

Seeing You

I see you in the flowers ~ as each petal starts to bloom....
and sense your spirit near me... as I'm sleeping in my room.
It doesn't take me very long to feel you anywhere ~
I've learned your spirit lingers close and find you everywhere.

I hear you in each lullaby that every robin sings ~
You're in the sky, the sea, and air .. and all that nature brings.
I never feel alone outside.. if I just close my eyes....
and listen to each small child's laugh ~ you never really died.

We all live on in God's great plan... our souls are near and bright ~
We'll see you glowing softly in each beauty of the night.
God's plan is so miraculous; and no one else can know...
the 'Mighty Joys' God has for us ~ we never really 'go'.

One day my time will end here... and my spirit will be free ~
to be so close to everyone ~ I wait in faith, to see.
What joys our God has planned for us... so great to comprehend ~
Our lives are held in His sweet arms and never really end.

Diane Ranker Riesen

Send a Star

I have so many perfect friends ~ and some live far away....
before I lay me down to sleep .. I have a prayer to say.
Although we cannot always see each other face to face ~
love transcends all distance and travels everyplace.

"Dear Lord, protect my loved ones... hold them tightly in Your care;
let them know how dear they are; and that I'm always there.
Pick a special star for them ~ a star to fill their night....
and let them feel the love I send with this sweet "Holy Light".

May all Your peace surround them ~ may You cover them with grace...
as each star sends them warmness, and sparkles on their face.
I can sleep much better now .. just knowing You have heard ~
my special prayer of love to them - I know You'll bless each word!"

Diane Ranker Riesen

Sheltered

Oh, how great to know we're sheltered ~ in a world that holds much pain;
such a joy to feel protected from the turmoil, hurt, and rain.
This world is filled with boundless beauty - such love is everywhere ~
but when some evil strikes to hurt us...We have a God that's always there.

I can't imagine life without Him ~ such a futile way to live-
to think there's nothing after death; and nothing more to get or give.
When the world gets overwhelming; and you feel that all is lost.....
remember God is always listening- He saved our lives at every cost.

Try to take the harder days; and find a way to spread some joy —
find a place where you can sit and see some beauty to enjoy.
Thank you, God... I know we'll make it; ~~ with Your Power by our side...
Eternity will last forever ~ such peace to know we never 'die'.

Diane Ranker Riesen

Sights Beheld

Good Morning, Lord, I see the sun that's filled with all Your light ~
and know, that in the evening, I'll see wonders of Your night.
How powerful Thy hands must be - what majesty You hold....
that brings such glorious beauty in the sights that we behold.

What kind of King can rule the skies, and turn the rain to snow ~
what power lies within Your hands ~ too much for us to know.
Each luscious meadow filled with green; and every shining star....
shouts out the glory of Your Power, and everything You are.

A snow capped mountain stately stands ~ and oceans ebb and flow;
such countless proof that You exist, with each celestial show.
How can one wonder if You're real? How can there be a doubt ~
when all the world sings out Your Power, and all its wonders shout?

I stand in awe with each new day; and wait in anxious stance ~
to watch the melodies of life, and watch each flower dance.
Thank you, God ~ for all Your gifts… how plentiful You show ~
the kind of power You control ~ too much for us to know.

And then when days are numbered ~ and this earth becomes anew…
Your Powers will magnify our sights ~ Your words will all come true.
In Heaven we will feel such peace, and beauties so unknown ~
We'll be surrounded by Your Love ~ and never be alone.

Diane Ranker Riesen

Sleep Wishes

If I could have some wishes.. that would come true for one night;
I'd turn into a lightning bug ~ and take an evening flight.
I'd flash my light with joyful glee under a willow tree ~
and smile as all the children tried to run and capture me.

I'd also be a butterfly ~ with wings of glorious hues…
and try to place myself within a thousand different views.
My wings would spread out widely; and float upon the air ~
and I could have the perfect spot to see love everywhere.

I'd like to be a tiny bird ~ all cuddled in a nest….
and feel the warmth surrounding me while I lay down to rest.
My time there would be very short ~ for I would have to learn…
how to fly all by myself and take my place, in turn.

What about a flower, oh I long to be a rose ~
and stretch up to the sunshine, as gentle breezes blow.
My scent would be exquisite ~ as it lifted in the air….
And live within a garden; with children playing near.

I could go on for hours ~ there's so many gorgeous things.
It'd be so great to witness them and hear all nature 'sing'.
I'll save these wishes for my dreams ~~~ and when I go to sleep~
I'll store each memory somewhere safe; so I can always 'keep'.

Diane Ranker Riesen

Sleep

Guard our hearts from Heaven's throne ~
keep us sheltered as Your own...
bless each dream that comes our way;
Prepare us for the coming day.

May Your Spirit hover close ~
You're the One we need the most.
As we slumber through the night...
keep us in Your Holy sight.

How blessed we are to have You, Lord ~
from Your Hand.... our blessings pour.
And when we wake to greet the sun...
our hearts be filled with all You've done.

Diane Ranker Riesen

Sleeping Babe

Oh what tender tears were shed ~ when first I lay my babe to bed...
My heart so full with purest love.... as God sent angels from above.
There are no words to share the sight - as softly my child entered night -
I prayed sweet dreams would show their way... as he slept gently; till the day.

I stared in awe upon his face... this sweet and perfect soul ~
He filled my soul with purpose... and made perfection whole.
Each night I find it hard to leave ~ his room brings me such peace;
as all the world seems better; and all my problems cease.

One day these times will dwindle ~ as he grows to be a man....
Until you have your own small babe... no one can understand.
Heaven visits me each night as I stand in that room ~
"Stay small awhile, my baby boy.... Please dare not grow too soon".

Diane Ranker Riesen

Slumber

Oh, tonight ~ what gentle comfort.....
knowing You are always there.
Such peace inside my soul tonight ~
knowing You will always care.

As we lay to slumber softly....
I pray so deeply for my friends.
As You listen so intently ~
such pure love that never ends.

May this sleep be filled with rainbows....
Shining stars, and whispered 'love'.
We below are covered tightly ~
by Your Spirit from above.

Diane Ranker Riesen

Snow Wings

I looked outside my window ~~ and this is what I found....
a cushioned, fluffy, powdered sugar blanket on the ground.
What sense of peace it gave me...as I stared out on the view ~
And knew the Winter Wonderlands had started to come true.

Winter brings such coldness — with chills and blustering winds....
the heated days of Summer are all gone once it begins.
But every season has its time and each has unique powers....
Winter has its snowflakes, just as Summer has its flowers.

I anxiously await each time... each season brings such sights ~
And oh the view of glistening snow on dark and star-filled nights.
I love the gleam of dripping ice ~ that hangs upon the trees...
embrace each wondrous picture ~ and enjoy them - such as these.

One very simple miracle that happens every year-
is what I find within the snow - from children that I hear.
I look outside, once children leave, and my soul starts to sing.....
They left their mark out in the snow .. with countless Angel Wings!

Diane Ranker Riesen

Soft Night

Angels' Wings around my head ~
Heavenly songs surround my bed....
Nothing sad can stay so wrong -
when you keep 'Faith' secured and strong.

Let the darkness comfort you ~
feel God's power through and through.
Rest your thoughts and calm your soul...
let God's warmth surround you 'whole'.

Sometimes 'NIGHT's the only time ——
when all your senses feel in rhyme.
Enjoy the quiet, peace filled night ~
until the early morning light.

Diane Ranker Riesen

Some Day

Opalescent droplets of God's tears pouring down ~
is what I think of all the rain that falls upon the ground.
God loves us unconditionally ~ and His heart truly breaks....
when each of us are suffering, He hurts for our pains sake.

It's hard to understand why God won't take away each pain ~
He has the might and power to erase the hurtful rain—
but with free 'Will' God's hands are tied... He cannot interfere ~~~
with the consequences following some choices man's made here.

Our world is torn and tainted... by mistakes along the way ~
but we will see a world renewed; and free of sin one day.
Heaven waits for each of us ~ the world God meant for me....
my mind can't comprehend the perfect glory I will see.

And so, till then, we need to try to cherish days on earth ~
and do whatever we can do to salvage love and worth.
Some days will be much harder ~ but God's with us all the way....
until we finally reach God's home... until we see that day!

Diane Ranker Riesen

Star Filled Night

How precious can an evening be ~
when I lay down beneath a tree;
and gaze my vision up to the skies....
I wait for answers to my 'whys'.

The stillness makes such time for prayer ~
as I lay silent.... waiting there.
The stars are scattered through the night,
and make a profound, perfect sight.

How do they stay and twinkle ~
with such a perfect glow?
Their majesty is far beyond..
all other lights I know.

I pray in silence down below ~
the mystery of God's mighty 'show'.
How powerful my God must be...
to make the stars, and all I see.

Questions grow.... while my eyes stare ~
at all the beauty showing there.
My mind can't fathom all I see...
I feel so small beneath that tree.

I prayed for God to let me know...
what glory lies beyond His 'show'....
and in that instant ~ sent from 'far'...
my eyes beheld a 'shooting star'!

God's answers can be found so clear...
if we just look and we just hear.
His signs of power are all around~
in every sight and every sound.

As I lay 'neath that towering tree~
I feel God's love surrounding me.
And though, I'll never know just 'how'....
I lay content ~~ with proof ~~~ for now.

Diane Ranker Riesen

Strengthen Me

In such this early dawning ~ as my eyes begin to wake....
I feel the need to speak to You - before my teardrops break.
I'm getting better every day - and know You keep me strong.
Although I fear the day ahead ~~, with You, it won't be wrong.

Early morning moments are a chance to Bless your day ~
just whisper hopeful thoughts to God... He'll hear the words you say.
God longs for this sweet time with you - His Spirit overflows....
all those secret worries hidden, ... He already knows.

And when you reach out to your King ~ in pure and simple need...
He'll cherish all your faith in Him, and secure your every plea.
Oh joyous morning moments ... relish every blessing sent ~
Your time with God will always be the best you ever spent.

Diane Ranker Riesen

Strong Faith

One day when I have long since gone ~ I hope my years show true...
that having Faith throughout my life was what helped get me through.
I've weathered storms of sorrows; and conquered days of strife ~
but holding on, and trusting God is how I got through life.

The sorrows will diminish and the pain will also 'dim';
just keep on trusting and hold on ~ give these days to 'Him'.
God never wanted any of us to endure such painful hours....
but consequences follow men ~ and we must handle 'ours'.

I've found that every time I make it through another pain ~
that God was right there with me and great lessons I had gained.
I'd rather have the perfect days, when all the world is right....
but sin steals so much happiness... we have to stand and fight!

When you awake with burdens that are weighing down on you...
and you assume that for that day there's nothing you can do ~~~
Remember there's a Higher Power that supersedes the way ~
and call on Him to intercede, and brighten up your day.

I promise God will hear you ~ and answer all your needs....
we have to realize God's always watching, and He sees ~
that everything will work out ~ according to His Plans.
God had a pathway clearly drawn before the birth of man.

I pray we lean back on our strengths and offer up our pleas ~
and trusting God will guarantee He'll give us what we need.
Our time on earth has challenges, and some days seem so wrong....
But we can conquer every trial if we keep our faith strong.

Diane Ranker Riesen

Stumbles

To wake up with a ray of hope ~
and know you'll have some strength to cope;
is what we all strive hard to keep...
through sorrows, stumbles, wake, and sleep.

Some days don't work out as we plan;
and it seems hard to understand ~~~~
But with a Faith that stays secure...
our hearts can bear what 'pains' endure.

How wonderful it would be to know...
How every hour and day would go ~
but that's just not the way Life is...
We need to know our life is "His".

Whenever something goes astray ....
and darkness tries to steal our day:
be quiet, still, and say a prayer ~
God's wide awake and always there.

Some days may not be as you planned ~
but don't give up ~ lift up and stand.
Tomorrow brings a whole new day.
And 'Hope' is always 'here' to stay.

Diane Ranker Riesen

Sun

Dear Sun, I feel you shining.... so warmly on my face ~
each flower opens widely, and I see life everyplace.
Dear Birds, I hear you singing... while perched up in the tree ~
I feel your song is perfect; and you're singing just for me!

How special is the morning... when we all can start anew-
we each can change our lives around; and pray for me and you.
Remember every morning, as those glorious rays abound....
that each day is so precious ~ with new beauties all around.

Oh Sun and birds keep blessing us ~ with signs of Heaven's truth...
and may I never stop to recognize each gift from you.
Greet the day with happiness ~ embrace each hour with love....
God's smiling down from Heaven as He watches from above!

Diane Ranker Riesen

Surely

Surely, float up in the air~
find your peace with God up there.
No more trials and no more pain;
completely free and 'whole' again.

Oh, if I could see you then….
better than you've ever been!
But 'faith' must be my proof for now ~
in humble thanks.. I pray and bow.

Thank you, God… for what we'll see ~
when we leave for 'eternity'.
Until that time, please give us peace…
until the time our souls release.

Earth holds such beauty ~ let me see…
the countless joys You've made for me -
the glories that Your hands have done….
will show me hints of what's to come!

Diane Ranker Riesen

Sweet Kisses

Sweet kisses of this night time breeze ~
Blow gently, ….heal my worries, please.
And sparkling drops of moonlight reach….
to give my soul such sweet release.

As I lay down to rest my soul ~~~
the evening makes me softly whole.
And all the world begins to dream -
Within the moonlight's gentle beam.

Diane Ranker Riesen

Sweet Sleep

Guard our hearts from Heaven's throne ~
keep us sheltered as Your own…
bless each dream that comes our way;
prepare us for the coming day.

May Your Spirit hover close ~
You're the one we need the most.
As we slumber through the night….
keep us in Your Holy Sight.

How blessed we are to have You, Lord ~
from Your hand… our blessings pour.
And when we wake to greet the sun…
our hearts be filled with all You've done.

Diane Ranker Riesen

Sweet Spirit

Oh, my soul, so filled with wordless joy ~~~
My Father's Spirit dwells within me strong -
my arms outstretched in glory....
I'm right where I belong.

Each sacred tune of Heaven's choir..
is whispered in my ears ~~~~
as God's blanket of protection....
dismantles every fear.

I pray tonight securely known...
until my slumber starts ~~~
that God will cradle each of you,
and glow within your hearts.

Diane Ranker Riesen

Sweetness

Oh, how the evening teases me ~ with all its peaceful feel;
it taunts me every night now - and nothing else seems real.
The perfect moonlit shadows… that dance upon the ground ~
mesmerize my senses like no other time around.

I plan to sit, just for a while…. and breathe the nightly air ~
but once I start to view the sights ~ I continue staying there.
Describing what this does for me; is hard to put in words…..
the different songs that comfort me… the chirping of the birds.

One must take time to see this joy ~ it brings such calm and peace….
and while I sit and watch the scenes, my soul finds such release.
Thank you, Evening, for your gift … renewing me each night ~
until the darkness slowly fades within the morning light.

Diane Ranker Riesen

Talents

I can climb a willow tree and sit out on its branch....
I can stand out in the rain, and even start to dance.
There are so many options; and so many ventures, too ~
but there are things more difficult ~ that I can never do.

I can rock a baby, and stop its troubling cry....
or stand out in a meadow; and watch a bluebird fly.
But I can't make that precious babe, or give a bird its wings ~
I can't make the raindrops start, or make the sparrows sing.

I'm grateful for the gifts I have ~ and all I get to do....
I know that God's the reason why we have these blessings, too.
Yet even with the many things that our minds learn and share ~
there's no way all the things we do could ever dare compare.....
    to the wonders of our Mighty God and what His Powers possess-
    He's the Maker of the Universe, the stars, and all the rest.

Our talents are so limited ~ and we could never know.....
all the wonders of our Mighty God, and how He makes things grow.
    Life and nature come from God ~ all vision and each breath...
    and only God ordains our fate, and knows our timely death.
We need to use the gifts we have ~ but always be aware.....
that God's the only reason why these gifts are even there.

Diane Ranker Riesen

Tender Mercies

Oh, that clouds would cover me ~
like a blanket; heavenly....
and stars surrounding ... by my bed;
with tender moon glow on my head.

What sweet sleep - I would be blessed...
as I lay down to my rest.
God's mercies never leaving me ~
with His sweet arms protecting me.

Thank you, Lord, for kindness shown...
while in the night I'm not alone.
I sense You always close to me ~
I sleep in peace .. with worries freed.

Diane Ranker Riesen

Thankful Tears

Tonight I'll sleep much better.. than the night I did before ~
I'm pushing out my sad thoughts, and I'm locking up the door.
The absolutely best thing I could ever do —- is PRAY....
so I'll keep my worries locked and then they can't get in my way.

No one else can find the answers like Our God Above ~
no one else cares more for sorrow ~ no one holds more love...
and, with that truth ingrained in me, my soul can be at peace -
I'll feel the joy He promises ~ while all my worries cease.

Of course, I'll wake and take them back - just like I always do....
but deep inside I know, again - I'll hand them back to You!
Thank you, Lord ~ for loving me enough to calm my fears ~
as I can then sleep 'sweet and sound'... through every thankful tear.

Diane Ranker Riesen

The Answers

Oh, how my heart aches so.. for you ~ I wish I could do more….
You've been so burdened through the years; with the sorrows you have bore.
It doesn't make much sense to me ~ that your life has been so rough….
and I wonder when our God will raise His Hand and say "enough!".

There seems to be no rhyme to all the heartache you have seen…
Some lives go by so smoothly… with so little 'hurt' between ~~~~
but then there are the ones who seem to struggle through each year;
just when things seem to just improve.. new sorrows soon appear.

Why does this often happen… when no one deserves such pain?
I pray to God for answers ~ when I'm wondering once again.
They say you're never given any more than you can take —
but why are some so loaded down… until they almost 'break'?

I know the answer lies in "Faith" … but strength can disappear ~
those times when all your soul is lost, and you can't feel 'God' near….
I've come to realize my mind's so small and can't compare —
to all the truths God holds inside; and why things seem unfair.

In times so hard that Faith seems weak ~ I look back on the cross..
God's Son deserved a perfect life; but, He also paid such cost.
I have no answer here on earth.. no reasons will seem fair ~~~
but 'Faith' is what will comfort me - Heaven holds the answers 'there'.

Diane Ranker Riesen

The Boy

I was thinking of these darkened times …in a world so lost of joy ~
when I felt somebody close behind - I turned and saw this boy.
His smile was so contagious; as he softly said "hello"…
and then he spoke with gentle sound.."There's something you should know."

I don't know where he came from ~I'd been walking all alone….
but within just minutes with him, I felt 'hope' I'd never known.
He said he saw me by myself and felt the need to talk ~
He began to tell a story.. as we moved along our walk.

"I'm walking home from school right now, and today was very sad ~~~
the boy that always eats with me was the best friend that I had.
But he did not show up today ~ and my teacher told the class….
that Bobby's heart was very weak- and it just couldn't last.
I'm trying hard to understand ~ why God would let this be…
when his parents came to get his things ~ there was something left for me."

I saw that he was holding a sealed letter in his hand…
but hadn't had the strength to read that letter from his friend.

"Do you think that you could stay with me as I read what Bobby wrote?
I just don't want to be alone …. when I saw you, Jesus spoke.
He told me you were here for me, and Jesus felt my need ~
to have someone beside me."

Then he began to read……

'I just really want to thank you ~ for being my best friend….
and even on our bad days - you helped me even then.

Diane Ranker Riesen

I have a heart that doesn't work the way it really should ~
but even on my weaker days… you made me feel so good.

I never spoke about it ~ I know you never knew….
I just wanted our pure friendship to stay normal around you.
But, if you get this letter ~ then, you know I've gone away.
My parents knew to give you this on one specific day.'

I stood in awe, beside this boy ~ as he read the words out loud;
He didn't want to be alone… but, didn't want a crowd.
I knew that God had placed me there, within this small boy's sight ~
and what he taught me on that day ~ made everything seem right.

'You made me feel so special, and you helped me feel so good….
even on the rotten days ~ I always knew you would.
So, thank you, friend ~ for being .. so caring till the end;
and when I'm gone, I'll send some little gifts to you, my friend.

Each time you grin ~ I'll be there; and I'll love to see your smile ~
and every day, I'll stay real close, and be there all the while.
Just keep on living every day and see the good around ~~~
in everything you see and know - there's so much joy around.'

He closed the note up neatly… then, he looked into my eyes ~
I tried to be supportive; as I softly smiled and cried.
He promised me he'd listen to the words his friend had said….
and try real hard to notice good; and ignore the bad, instead.

He said his house was just ahead, and thanked me for my time ~
Bobby changed his life that very day ~ and he, in turn, changed mine.
No longer will I linger on the sadness all around….
or dwell on all the sad things ~ there's joy that can found.

Who was this little boy I met? .. and why did he choose me?
I think my eyes were blinded ~ and he taught me how to see....
that even though great heartaches come - and things can get me down....
I'll close my eyes, and see that boy ~ and find joy all around.

Diane Ranker Riesen

The Christmas Star

The Christmas Star will soon shine bright~
to guide the Magi Kings that night...
and, lo, the stillness of the view~
to see our Christ Child beaming new.

What glory shown, in perfect peace;
as choirs of Angels never cease~
to sing the birth of our new King....
the Heavens filled as angels 'sing'!

And as the star began to fade...
the newborn King, divinely made.....
was here to save the fate of man~
and then - salvation's gift began.

What wondrous gift our God released...
to know His own Son would decease.
And from that meager manger cold -
would fulfill the greatest story told.

Diane Ranker Riesen

The Cure

Hello, dear Lord ~ I pray to Thee......
Give me eyes that I may 'see' ~
every blessing sent my way;
and how You love me every day.

Direct my vision to Your view......
that I may cherish what You do.
Sometimes, I just forget to say....
a joyful 'thanks' for gifts today.

Thank you, God, for being here ~
I pray to feel Your Spirit near....
and then I know my life's secure -
and all my soul seems full and pure.

Diane Ranker Riesen

The End

One day, when my life's reached its end ~ and I gaze through the years....
I hope I 'gave' more than I 'got' ... and smiled throughout the tears.
Each day is such a special gift - God has so much to show......
I pray I've learned some wondrous truths - with each year that I grow.

A tiny flower can teach me strength... when dryness haunts the land;
Although it struggles with the thirst - rain helps it stand again.
Each creature needs some shelter, and sometimes the wind blows cold...
but somehow God provides for each; and 'surviving power' takes hold.

When I'm gone and leave this earth - I pray for memories....
of joy-filled hours and wondrous days... that I can take with me.
There's nothing more important than the love you give away;
or times you've helped another .. with the kind words that you say.

Lord, take my life and use it ... may I show Your blessings full ~
and never may I doubt that I have showed "YOU" in my soul.
If I can live my life like this ~~~ I'll know I've filled each day..
and then, return back home to You ~ and hear Your gentle praise.

Diane Ranker Riesen

The Flight

Some nights the skies seem brighter; and I've guessed the reason why…….
'I imagine extra angels have taken to the sky.'   ~~~~~
Their brilliance and their glory cast a beauty through the stars ~
and I sense a perfect calmness as they travel where they are.

I say a prayer and raise my eyes - and think I see some wings ~
and ponder all the blessings .. and hear the heavens sing.
Our final journey's not the end ~ it's really just the start…..
nothing can erase our love and keep us far apart.

Enjoy the glory, jump the clouds, and hug those waiting there ~
A brand new life is starting without burdens, hurt, or care.
One day, I hope I light the sky ~ I'd dance among the stars….
and watch you all from Heaven… and know right where you are!

Diane Ranker Riesen

The Gift

Amidst this morn of Christmas noise ~
the laughter, smiles, and children's toys....
enjoy the glee of cheerful joy -
Yet don't forget one baby boy.

For God foresaw our futures full -
and Only He could fully know....
that we would need some help one day ~
to save the world and show the Way.

As hearts beat full with family love ~
remember what was sent above....
the most important gift this morn -
Our Saviour, Jesus Christ, was born!

Diane Ranker Riesen

The Mighty Sky

Stars align in darkness.. to brighten up the night ~
and once again God lets me know that things will be alright.
Our planet still spins perfectly within such darkened space…
and one more time I know for sure… that God is everyplace.

Sometimes my doubts encumber me, and cause my 'praise' to slow….
but, soon enough my Mighty God will give me proof to show -
that nothing ever goes unseen, God knows of all my pains ~~~
He lifts His Hand and shakes the skies, and helps my faith again.

How dare I even question life ~ or ponder why things change…..
God has always led the way….. His Power always reigns.
A small and tiny planet — floating magically in air ~~
is just more proof and guarantee that God is always there.

Our universe so large and vast… unparalleled by none……
is guarded and protected by my God, the Mighty One.
Whenever worries taunt me ~ or my soul begins to fear…
I glance into the night time skies, and know that He is here.

Diane Ranker Riesen

The Nest

I woke up to a miracle ~ outside my window sill....
I saw the perfect power, and the plan of God's sweet "will".
I've looked outside each day now- when I awoke from rest-
to see a lovely bluebird sitting stately on her nest.

I only caught her eggs alone... a couple times at most-
She'd rarely leave all through the day, and stayed there at her post.
This morning though, seemed different than each one I saw before ~
This bluebird perched up higher; and I could see some more.

Just as I was marvelling at what nature provides...
her tiny eggs began to ever slightly move inside.
Then, just a tiny crack appeared, but I was stuck in awe ~
I stayed there by my window, and cried at what I saw.

Her babies were awakening and breaking through their shells,
a proud mom watched, and I sat still, so quietly .. until....
all five of her sweet baby birds had poked out ~ I could see ~
They'd entered nature one by one, and it astonished me!

How perfect can God's power show the magic of His plan...
I witnessed such perfection; and the power of His Hand.
And then the mother softly placed her body close to each
I learned that morning what amazing things nature can teach.

I left my room to start my day... remembering that sight -
and knew I'd see more miracles all day until the night.
Never forget to keep your eyes wide open to each view....
there are a million miracles that happen all day through.

Diane Ranker Riesen

The Only One

Sometimes God answers quietly ~
sometimes it's in a "roar"....
But I will wait and trust Him,
just like I've done before.

Sometimes His answer seems so wrong ~
and though it breaks my heart...
He knows my life in full now,
so I'll trust Him from the start.

This doesn't mean I do not cry ~
and I can't understand....
But He is master of it all -
and has a perfect plan.

I hope your prayers are answered...
in a soft and gentle way ~
and pray His peace will comfort you -
throughout each single day.

When answered prayer just seems so wrong...
and you're put to the test ~~~~
Remember God's the only One
who REALLY knows what's best.

Diane Ranker Riesen

The Other Side of the Rainbow

On the other side of the rainbow…. the sky is always blue -
there are no storms or thunder ~ nor rainfall to walk through.
There's stunning beauty everywhere, and colors never known…
all the dreams you wondered ~~ are finally being shown.

On the other side of the rainbow…. the flowers sing in tune ~
they never dry and whither ~~ they always stay in bloom!
And all of nature welcomes you.. with greens, and pinks, and browns ~
with gorgeous views of wonder ~ where God's great gifts abound.

On our side of the rainbow… each season has an end ~
so many sights we witnessed ~ ~ we'll never see again.
But never on the other side - for there's no time nor space….
and we keep all our memories… they live there 'everyplace'.

On our side of the rainbow ~ each year we age and 'slow' ~
our bones begin to weaken… and we no longer grow.
But oh what perfect futures are awaiting us one day….
where nothing ever harms us, and 'love' is all that stays.

On the other side of the rainbow… every wish you had comes true -
and all your loved ones gather near ~ to always stay with you.
Heaven lies just there beyond - and one day we will see….
all the joys our 'faith' secured ~ in our 'eternity'!

Diane Ranker Riesen

The Same

Each week, each month… each year has passed ~
and I'm still hurting ~~ like the last.
I've built a tolerance to my pain….
but I still miss you just the same.

Some say that it gets easier ~ that time will ease your scar….
but the truth is grief is endless… and, it changes who you are.
Sometimes the pain is not as sharp ~ your soul learns how to 'bare'…..
but that emptiness down deep inside your heart is always there.

There'd be no grief without such love - and, so I'll carry on ….
Your memories are worth it all … they've helped me since you're gone.
And through my faith I truly know that one day you'll be here —
right here, beside me .. like before ~ and my questions will be cleared.

Till then I'll see you in my dreams… and watch you in my mind ~
although time takes so much from me - my memories will be kind.
And in those special moments when I still can feel you close…..
is where I'll find contentment - when I'm missing you the most.

Diane Ranker Riesen

The Time

His days are shortly numbered, Lord ~ please take him by Your Hand….
Take Him Home if that's Your Will, and help us understand.
We're so attached to earthly things that often we don't see ~~
there's so much more just waiting - when our souls are finally 'free'!

Let him dance upon Your stars… and slide down on Your moon ~
May Angels bless him with a song that's filled with Heaven's 'tune'.
It's hard to just imagine… what happens when we die ~
but with Your Promise to us ~ I'm always going to try.

I miss the ones who leave me… I miss their face and smile ~
but comfort comes whenever I think ~ they're through with pain and trial.
Oh, may he walk through meadows filled with Heaven's special scent -
and may he be so blessed by You.. he's happy that she went!

I'll wait upon Your plan for me ~~ and while I'm living here….
I'll keep You close in humble prayer and know You're always near.
And when the angels come for me.. with love to take me home ~
I'll have those loved ones with me - closer than I've ever known.

Diane Ranker Riesen

THE VALIANT
- Our service men and women -

I dare not follow in your steps; nor trudge your wearied miles ~
My eyes can't bear the sights you've seen - 'unselfish' all the while.
I fear my soul would disappear… my heart would break in two -
if I would truly feel the pain and sorrows you went through.

Your courage, strength, and bravery can never be repaid…
You faced the worst this world can do ~ while we stayed safe and 'prayed'.
Such tortured days ~ none can compare…. your valiant gift to all ~
You gave those years in honor.. so our country would not fall.

Such gratitude ~ such thankfulness… we honor you with pride -
to those who came back home to us, and to the ones who died.
We will remember always; and our thanks will never end….
to all of you who suffered ~ we praise your help, my friend.

Diane Ranker Riesen

The Waiting

Sometimes the "wait" seems endless ~
and each day is far too long.
I want the problem solved right now;
but everything seems wrong.

Problems seem relentless -
with no solution clear in sight.
I want so bad to fix it,
and I want to make it right.

But that's not how the world works -
and I have to trust God's plan.
I need to lift it all in prayer ~
and know God understands.

Deep in my soul I know it's true….
but my 'human' side gets weak ~
and I falter in my faithfulness
when things get really bleak.

But what a comfort knowing….
that God is always close ~
And He can understand my faults,
just when I need Him most!

In God's time everything will change ~
and, in His arms… I'll wait.
He's known before the earth began,
He's always known each fate.

Diane Ranker Riesen

These Hours

On this night of saddened hearts, tear-stained cheeks and darkened clouds....
we all must pause and say a prayer, 'love' each other - say "out loud" ~
.... for anger grew here once again, and tore a hole deep in our hearts ...
we cannot let this evil win ~ or try to tear us all apart.

Nothing good will ever come.. from hardened souls, or damaged dreams....
we must stay strong and fight the wrong ~ keep our 'Faith' by any means.
Though the pain and hurt burns high.. and the bitterness stays strong ~
we must stand firm in kind repose - knowing evil's always wrong.

Fold our hands on bended knee ~ as we lay our day to rest.....
look to God for comfort shown - only He can ease this test.
No evil action, thought, or foe.... can crush God's mighty power ~
we will ever cling to Him - to calm us through these hours.

Diane Ranker Riesen

This Little Boy

I was having such a rotten day; and feeling pretty low ~
when suddenly a small boy stopped…. 'Someone I didn't know'.
His mother said his friendliness would scare her some at times….
he never knew a stranger, and he sometimes crossed the line.

I smiled at her and let her know that I was glad to see…….
this little child with such a grin - decide to come to 'me'.
He told me that he noticed I was sitting all alone ~
and wanted just to say 'hello'.. . to 'ME' , he'd never known!

I thanked him for his sweetness; and I gave his mom a 'wink'….
I felt there was a reason why he came to me, I think.
Some days just seem so endless, and I just felt all alone ~
but this boy made me smile and laugh with all the care he'd shown.

Such tiny little gestures…. can open up your heart ~
he came up close and hugged me right before he went to part.
And as he walked away from me - a tear swelled in my eyes,
I felt so blessed that I had met this tiny little guy.

Who was this little boy I met?.. and why did he choose me?
I think my eyes were blinded ~ and he taught me how to see….
that even though great heartaches come, and things can get me down ~
I'll close my eyes, and see that boy ~~ and find 'joy' all around!

Diane Ranker Riesen

This Love

I didn't think that I could love… the way I love my child.
I never thought my heart would melt to see "perfection" mild.
I hadn't even held you yet ~ you just arrived 'brand new';
But something changed inside of me the second I saw you.

Some love is based on feelings that can change from day to day ~
but my love for you was different ~ and unique in every way.
So deep and unconditional… unlike I've ever known….
My soul was touched by heaven ~ the moment you were shown.

I vow to always cherish you; and always be aware ~
Of this precious gift God's given me ~ and shield your life in prayer.
I thought I knew how I would feel… and found that I was wrong -
'You' made my life worth living; and I know where I belong.

One day Our God will take us home ~ when each our lives are done…
God trusted me to raise you; and help you to become ——
the faithful child He molded ~ and sent here for awhile~
I'll help you through each year of life; and guide you through each trial.

Diane Ranker Riesen

This Night, Lord

Tonight I thank You, Father, for each blessing I hold dear ~
and pray for Mighty mercies for the sorrows we have here.
There is no power greater ~ nor another Holy King...
who can solve the worries of this world ~ such gratitude I sing!

Thank you for my loved ones, whether family, friend, or foe ~
each has added lessons to my life that I should know.
I honor You for loving me ~ and kneel in humble prayer...
no matter what is hurting me... I know that You are here.

I ask you, Lord, to heal the sick ~ and strengthen all the weak ~
I pray each soul finds Your 'living word'; and everything they seek.
I know that in this quiet night... Your Power will conquer sin;
and at the end of earthly days ~ each one of us will win.

Diane Ranker Riesen

Those Crosses

As I gaze upon the sights on my early morning drive ~
I take the time to pray... and thank God I'm alive.
For none of us are sure just when our days will end.....
I get reminded daily of 'loss' around the bend.

Along a dusty road - I see some flowers near.....
and then I see the 'cross' that I so deeply fear.
Someone had lost a loved one along that road one day ~
and the cross is our reminder that someone went away.

Each time you happen by a simple, wooden cross ~
please say a single prayer for the person who was lost.
For every life is precious and grief can steal so much.....
But every person leaves *'a very special touch'*.

Those crosses ever growing — they never seem to end ~
they stand as a reminder to *"watch around the bend"*.
Be safe in your endeavors ~ and always lift a prayer....
whenever you pass crosses ... each one so sweetly there.

Diane Ranker Riesen

Through the Dark

I've seen it happen time and again ~ just when I've lost all hope…
God sees my pain from Heaven, and He sends me help to cope.
You'd think I'd know by now that He will always help me through ~
but each time I am struggling ~ I forget He's with me, too.

When I am shaken to the core ~ and my mind gets so confused;
I need to keep my faith in tact…… and see what God will do.
Sometimes when I get broken; and my heart forgets what's true ~
I just get lost and forget, again ~ the magic God can do.

The next time I am hurting ~ and confusion blocks my mind…
God will always understand my faults; and He will take the time ~~~
to get me through the chaos and begin a brand new day.
When my Faith gets weak while things go wrong; my God will always stay.

Thank you, Lord, for loving me ~ and forgiving when I fall…
My mind will lose sight of the way…. but my soul remembers all.
In Your great wisdom You concede; and hear prayers I don't pray ~
When sorrow steals my power ~ I know You'll always stay.

Diane Ranker Riesen

Truths

Oh, what countless truths are shown...
what perfect timing so unknown ~
when nature's beauty still unfolds....
to show the Glory so untold.

How can a tree still startle me...
with every perfect leaf I see?
Its shade invites me there to rest ~
I love old, stately trees the best!

Right above my head so high.....
an eagle flies right through the sky.
Oh, how I wish to see its view ~
and see such sights I never knew.

There are so many treasures near....
I wish I could see each one clear.
Yet in God's time I'll see each one ~
below the moon, and in the sun.

I'll be content to wait each hour....
for God to show me every flower.
And, in the end, when time is through ~~~
my soul will have its greatest "view"!

Diane Ranker Riesen

Uncommon Pain

We cannot know God's reasonings; nor know what life has planned.
Sometimes the hurt is so intense ~ we'll never understand.
To lose a child is helpless, and we search so hard to 'ease'.....
but nothing really takes the hurt ~ it brings us to our 'knees'.

To lose another child would seem to be the cruelest pain ~
each loss just adds more heartbreak... and the sorrow starts again.
But few are called to bear the kind of suffering that will come ——-
when all the world seems hopeless, and you lose 'another' son.

I pray God sends a miracle to help the ones who've known....
this massive sense of sorrow that so few are ever shown.
Dear Father ~ use Your special care to help the ones who grieve ~
the ones who've had to stay behind, and watch their children leave.

There are no answers here on earth ... and weakness will take hold.
A parent's heart is torn in two ~ and all the world seems cold......
but there's a Faith that stands its ground, and will not ever leave ~
a strength God sends in darkest hours.. to those who just 'believe'.

We cry because we loved them, and each sibling just as much ~
Dear Father, send Your help to all... we need Your special 'touch'.
A parent's darkest nightmare will take many prayers and love....
until they're reunited with their children up above.

Diane Ranker Riesen

Understand

Oh Father, my Father ~ I just don't understand -
I'm on my knees for hours now... just praying for Your Hand.
It seems each day is endless; and I feel I've prayed so long ~
but everything just stays the same, and everything is wrong.

I'll never lose my Faith in You ~ I promised long ago ....
but why am I not answered?... please help for me to know.
Although it's true Your Knowledge reigns, and earthly minds are weak ~
this pain is overbearing, and relief is all I seek.

Then quietly... while on my knees ~ I heard a quiet sound —-

"Dear Child, I'm here right now with you ... I've always been around.
My knowledge knows each future day ~ and knows the path each takes.....
I'm working for your greater good... but know My heart still breaks.

You can't know what I know today... and, though I ache for you ~~~
Human 'Will' must have its power ~ please trust in what I 'do'.
I cannot bear your sadness, and I wish you knew the plan -
but till you get to where I'm at.. you just can't understand.

In each and every teardrop ~ through every breaking heart......
I stand along beside you, and will never be apart.
I know what happens in the end ~ yet, know your pain's so real ~
Rest your weary soul with Mine, and let Me help you heal."

Diane Ranker Riesen

Unselfish

Sometimes I feel so selfish ~ I do what's right for me....
but I know there are other places that I need to be.
It's just so easy to stay still... I need to try and change ~
God's hours can be different, and I must rearrange.

I have some people near me ~ who always spend each hour....
caring more for others, and sharing God's 'LOVE' power.
They're so unselfish with their time, and seem to always share -
everything they do each day is just because they care.

I want to be more like them ~ and try to give much more....
I want to do tomorrow what I didn't do before.
These people just amaze me ~ their souls divinely pure ~
if I could be more like them, I'd be better ~ that's for sure!

I give great thanks for each of you ~ you teach me every day....
how to better show my faith... you guide me on my way.
I know God sent you to me ~ God always has a plan ~
You're one of my sweet angels.... and now I understand.

Diane Ranker Riesen
(In tribute to Michael Frank, Tiffin, OH)

Use Me

There were so many times today ~ when I saw 'love' come by my way -
those precious moments caught my eye … a few so pure - they made me cry.
A tiny bunny struggled…. as it moved across my yard ~ ~
then, suddenly it's mom appeared, and tried so very hard
— to help her baby get back home, into its sweet, soft nest…….
and when they both arrived there ~ life was simply "at its best."

A little later, I was just relaxing in a chair ~
when I glanced up; and saw some children dancing in the air….
They giggled as they practiced all their movements perfectly -
and then one little girl stopped quick; and took a look at me.

She asked if I would like to join…. with cherub face so sweet ~
she'd noticed I was all alone, when she looked across the street.
I thanked her for her kindness ~ as I told her I must rest…
my tired legs were growing weak… but her sweetness was the 'best'!

I watched those children for some time ~ and returned a dozen waves….
they had no clue of all the simple happiness they gave -
what pure and joyous innocence shown brightly from their eyes ~
I blew a kiss to each of them as I said my goodbyes.

And now I lay down in my bed ~ and dwelt upon my day…..
when all at once my heart grew large, as I began to pray -
God let me know He visited in each thing that I viewed;
and that He shows Himself like that… my soul leaped with 'renew'!

God's everywhere and anywhere ~ He uses us to show….
the kind of love He so desires.. and He wanted me to know —

that every act of kindness, whether large or very small ~
is just a picture of the way He likes to use us all.

Diane Ranker Riesen

Use

God uses us in special ways that we can't understand ~
He knows each secret in us… we're created by His hand.
We each have certain talents that can help God in this life ~~
and it blesses us to use them~ to comfort others strife.

To give away the love you hold; and share each way you can…
has always been a factor in God's purpose for each man.
Sometimes it's such a simple thing that we easily lose sight ~
of all the power we possess… to help to make things right.

Take a second, slowly ~~ take a breath, and calm your mind -
you'll be amazed at all the strengths that you will feel and find.
Showing care and empathy to others who feel pain ~~~
will enrich your spirit deeply, and you'll want to help again!

Diane Ranker Riesen

Waiting

Oh! What joy my soul feels now ~~~
a pure and glorious touch -
I never knew it'd be like this....
Heaven holds so much!

Such happiness I've never known -
seen never in a dream ~
with love that fills my every breath;
and beauties never seen.

Our earthly death is just a door....
that opens Heaven's gate.
Never fear your ending....
but enjoy your earthly "wait"!

Diane Ranker Riesen

Waking

Time for sleep has now been through ~
the sun shines bright - and the sky is blue.
We waken to a brand new day...
it's time to yawn ~~~ be on our way!

The scent of roses fills the air -
with Heaven's blessings everywhere.
A little girl is skipping ~~ so sweetly all along...
while tender notes of music are scattered by her song.

How great it is to be each flower ...
each perfect growing tree —-
nature fills each precious morn ~
with countless creatures being born!

I keep my eyes wide open ~
so I will never miss....
the precious beauty God supplies
within these hours of bliss.

I choose to see the goodness ...
as I move along my walk ~
and cherish every friendship
that stops me quick ~~ to talk!

There is no time for sadness ...
when I glance up from my way ~
I see the countless miracles ...
God sends me every day!

Diane Ranker Riesen

Waves

Soft waves- splash gentle hugs on me ~ beyond the beach's view…..
and all the water's whispering sounds are, oh, so near me, too.
A little piece of Heaven ~ hid secretly below……
My respite from the busy world, and all the stress we know.

The soft, cool touch upon my skin — as Summer's heat shines down…..
No hectic rules can reach me here.. there's solace all around.
I find this spot, out in the blue - so peaceful, sweet, and pure ~
if you would try just once - this spot would capture you for sure.

Just give me several moments - time to relish where I am……
and then, in time, I will return… and love you once again.
Such wondrous waves of tenderness - recharge my inner soul ~
and I return back to the beach - refreshed and clearly whole.

Diane Ranker Riesen

Weak

Today, Oh Lord, I'm hurting ~~ I'm weak, lost, and confused;
all the strength I thought I had is gone; and has been used.
Each task seems overwhelming, and so useless to complete~
My spirit lives, but seems asleep ~~ I can't get on my feet.

Grief sneaks up out of nowhere, and it has no scheduled time....
It steals your breath and happiness ~ with no rhythm nor no rhyme.
Earth's trials seem so uncertain, and 'tomorrow' makes me shake...
for I have no idea how I'll feel when I awake.

Yet even in this darkness ~ there is 'faith' deep down inside...
and though it's weak and tired now .... Your Power will abide.
So in this weakened sorrow ~ I will say a single prayer;
and once again, fall back to You... and wait for answers there.

Diane Ranker Riesen

What Views

What wonders await us if we only took....
a moment each morning to just take a look.
All nature blooms softly ~ each miracle clear -
just open your eyes.. stop, listen, and hear.

Each tree shouts good morning through each waving leaf...
and miracles touch us ~~ if we just believe.
The soft clouds are billowing up in the air ~
take a moment to look ~ and see what is 'there'.

Each season is perfect ~ with gifts all their own...
the beautiful colors of change that are shown.
Oh, glorious flowers, and wonderful sights ~
with magical birds all perfect in flight.

Each time that we look ~ each time that we try....
we'll see different miracles filling our eyes.
How grateful our hearts should be to belong ~
in a world full of laughter, beauty, and song.

Let's try every morning ... to take in the view ~
there's much more awaiting than we ever knew......
and what a great treasure to start off our day -
by seeing the gifts that are lining our way!

Diane Ranker Riesen

Where Are the Miracles?

Show me a miracle, today, Oh Lord... I ask ~
I need to feel assurance ~~ something strong, so it will last.
So many random sorrows are surrounding us each day...
Your mighty truths are what I need to help me through the way.

So many prayers are lifted, every minute.. every hour -
people weak with illnesses who need Your Healing Power..
I look around and see such loss that sometimes I feel torn;
and feel my prayers aren't working; while so many grieve and mourn.

I want to SEE great miracles ~~ I want to SEE Your Power.....
too often I feel helpless as more people die each hour.
I really need some help from You... I pray You'll help me see ~
that every prayer I pray is heard, and that You intercede.

I'll close my eyes and listen, Lord ~ I'll wait so You can show....
that You are handling everything... I really need to know.
    I feel You coming closer now ~ my soul is opening wide;
    so I can hear Your answers; and feel Your truth inside.

"Dear child, I'm always listening .. and I hear each word that's prayed;
I know that healing's needed ~ and that no one wants delayed.
My mind sees everything in full... and yours can never know ~
why things seem so unanswered, and it's difficult to show.

Miracles abound each day—- they're right before your eyes -
many deaths denied by Me ~~~ go so unrecognized!
So many accidents appear, and death could have occurred.....
but I stepped in and saved their life... it's just nobody 'heard'.

Diane Ranker Riesen

A tiny baby makes it through another night of strife....
those prayers his parents sent to Me were heard; and saved his life.
There are signs ...every day from Me - I answer every prayer.....
but when a death occurs to them... 'My answer isn't 'fair'.

I want to reassure you that 'My Will' is for what's best ~~~~
and, when death rears its awful face, it puts 'faith' to a test.
But, when eternity is reached; and you can see My Way...
you'll understand the sorrows that your heart feels every day.

The losses will be understood ~ the healings will be shown.....
so many miracles occured that just were never known.
I love my children equally; and though earth's trials remain ~
I truly answer every prayer, and help you through each pain.

Just keep on holding onto Faith - remember I am near....
each prayer you pray is helping; and each single word I hear.
Blind faith can be so daunting; but, I promise in the end....
that you will see 'My Will' was true, and you will understand."

Diane Ranker Riesen

Where Are You?

Where are You, Lord, ... I'm looking ~
Where are You, Lord, ... I'm lost -
My mind is spinning recklessly;
my world is torn and tossed.

I have great 'Faith' within my heart ~
and though I'm sure You care....
I find myself so torn in two ~~~
and can't tell if You're there.

What do I do in times like these..
when troubles steal my mind?
I've tried to clear my senses....
I've searched, but cannot 'find'.

Then.. softly, in my soul ~~ I heard -
in My Lord's tender voice ......
"My child the world has been decayed ~
by human fault and choice.

Sometimes your mind will be consumed...
and you can't hear Me 'clear' ~
but never doubt that through those times —
I'm always very near.

Your Faith gives you the option ~~
to blindly trust My Power;
and even in those darkest times....
I'm with you every hour.

Diane Ranker Riesen

I'm sorry that the world is such…
that causes so much pain ~
but close your eyes and pray to Me…
I'll get you 'through' again."

Diane Ranker Riesen

Where I Belong

I watch each pain filled teardrop roll..so slowly down your face;
but KNOW those tears are for 'your' loss ~ I still am everyplace!
No earthly power anywhere… can ever end my soul…..
death has brought me freedom- and eternity is full.

I've known loss as you feel now; and I know that grief must 'be';
but understand I have no loss.. the love all came WITH me!
Do as you must to ease your pain. I know this hurt is real ~
but let it not surrender you to losing how we'd feel.

Until God calls you home to me - enjoy your earthly time….
Let death not steal the memories between your soul and mine.
For time is very limited, and years fly by so fast ~~~
It's hard for me to see you sad… our love will always last!

*****I wish I could appear to you
and prove I am not gone;
I've just returned to Heaven -
and I'm right where I belong.*****

Diane Ranker Riesen

Who Can?

Who can store some sunshine…. and keep it in a jar?
or reach up high to Heaven, and grab a piece of star?
I can hear the crickets play music in my ears……
but I can't call them to me - and make them just appear.

Can YOU count the blades of grass - that lay upon your yard?
~ or even count an inch of it… I think it would be hard!
Sweet raindrops fall upon my face in any given hour……
but I can't make that happen… there's just "ONE" who has that power!

Eagles are a marvelous view ~ as they streak across the sky….
but we have no control of them… nor gave them power to 'fly'.
All of nature turns in tune to God's almighty song ~~~~
everything in perfect place and just where they belong.

I feel so peaceful knowing….. that we're guarded by the best ~
I'm given strength to live each day.. through any trial or test.
Thank you, God…. for loving us; our souls are so secure….
with simple, childlike Faith in You… ETERNITY'S for sure!!!!!

Diane Ranker Riesen

Why Wait?

"My child, what are you waiting for ~
why are you so afraid?
My own Son took the pain for you...
your debts have all been paid..

What are you so afraid of?.....
Afraid you might be wrong?
Take a giant leap of Faith ~~
I'll help your soul get strong.

The fact that you are wondering..
is proof enough for ME ~~
that you are getting close to Me;
right now.... you just don't see.

All you need to do is ask ~~~
just open up the door.....
I'll prove within your spirit;
that I'm very real ~ and more.

Just do it now, and do not wait ~
there's much for you to feel.
In time, your heart and soul will know....
that I am very real!"

Diane Ranker Riesen

Wide Open

I need to keep my eyes wide open ~ I need to really 'see'.....
that when I think God doesn't hear me—- He IS answering me!
Too many times I just assume that if it's not MY way ~
then God was just too busy, and ignored the things I'd say.

But nothing could be farther from the truth of God's great plan -
He sees things from His throne of thrones, and we don't understand.
When prayers seem unattended ~ and you feel that God can't hear....
remember He feels everything — each triumph, pain, and fear.

His answer will come when it's time - His Knowledge reigns supreme...
and even in your darkest hours.. He's guarding every dream.
Faith is hard to cling to ~~~ when each hour just seems so wrong....
but God will have the final say - and He will keep you strong.

Diane Ranker Riesen

Worth the Pain

I always seem to dwell on all the times that I have lost ~
I think about the emptiness, and everything it's cost.....
But what if I decided to look back on all our time -
when things were right, and peaceful —-
                you were here, and you were mine!

I wish you stayed forever, and things never had to change....
but life is filled with twists and turns - and things get rearranged.
I'll never smile as happily ~ or feel such joy inside -
my world has changed forever since the moment that you died.

But would I give those moments up? .. and never had you near?
It takes me just a second, and then, suddenly ~ it's clear.....
Your loss was hard, and changed my life, but, oh so worth the pain~
you're gone for now, but in the end... I'll be with you again.

I wouldn't trade a second ~ and I'll cherish every day....
I'll try to keep the bitterness from getting in my way ~
I need to try much harder to be grateful you were here -
and, relish that I know you're ever peaceful, without fear.

Thank you, God, for gifting me with all those wondrous years ~
I'll try to honor such a joy... with laughter and not tears.......
for, all life ends at some point ~ but, eternity lives on -
I'll cherish every memory... till I reach where I belong.

Diane Ranker Riesen

Wrapped Wings

May the Angels gather 'round ~
to welcome babies "Heaven Bound"...
Wrap your wings around each child -
and sing sweet lullabies ~ so mild.

Such perfect souls were gone too soon....
Up beyond the stars and moon ~
Heaven's gates have opened wide -
to greet our 'blessings' that have died.

Too soon, and answers can't be known....
why we must face the days alone ~
But when we, too, meet in the skies....
God will answer all our 'why's?'..

Till then, sweet babies - now so blessed....
enjoy God's Love and all the rest ~~
You're safe and perfect where you are -
Our souls still near, and hearts not far.

What a joyous day will come ~
as we unite when time is done....
and then together we will share -
all God's glories shining there!

Diane Ranker Riesen

Year 2002

I lost you many years ago ~ and still nothing has changed....
all the times I thought we'd share.. were quickly rearranged.
I always thought we'd have much time.. but life can change so fast ~
and all the hours I thought we'd have just didn't seem to last.

I have a lot of memories ~ but I always wanted more.....
yet suddenly one afternoon my dreams were cracked and tore.
I've wondered endlessly for years why things had gone so wrong ~
most times I seem to handle things... but, I'm not always strong.

But then I stop and think of you and how you lived each day —
and through your great example ~ you've given me my way.
I'll try to see through your blue eyes and open up my ears ~~
I'll try to laugh as you did ~~~ and cherish all my years.

God had a special reason why He called you home so soon.
You sparkle up the stars each night and brighten up the moon ~
Stay where you are and relish every treasure you have now....
and when I get to where you are ~ you can teach me how.

Diane Ranker Riesen

Quotes by Diane Ranker Riesen

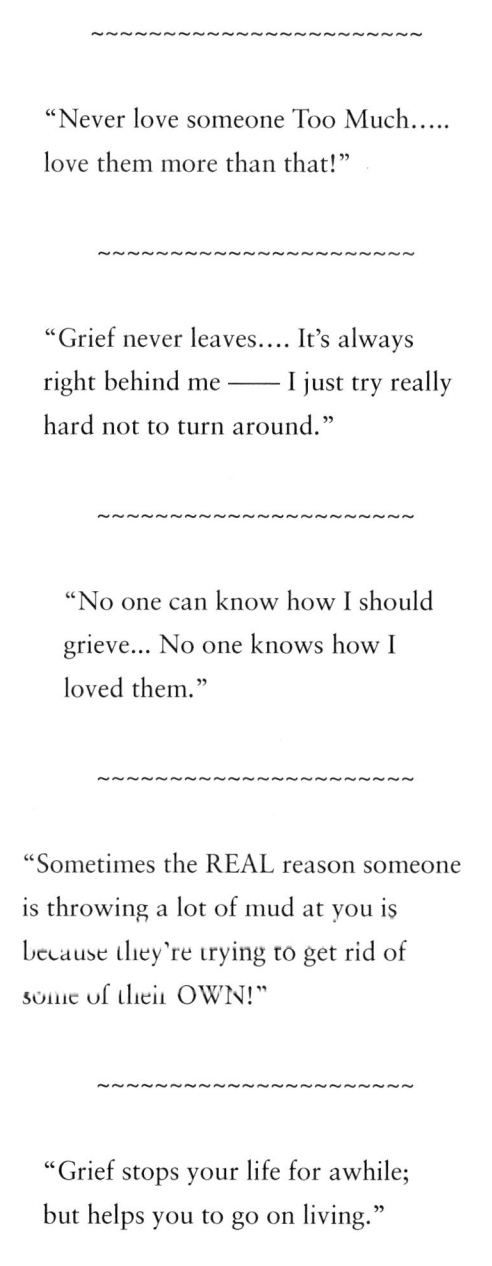

~~~~~~~~~~~~~~~~~~~~~~

"Never love someone Too Much…..
love them more than that!"

~~~~~~~~~~~~~~~~~~~~~~

"Grief never leaves…. It's always right behind me —— I just try really hard not to turn around."

~~~~~~~~~~~~~~~~~~~~~~

"No one can know how I should grieve… No one knows how I loved them."

~~~~~~~~~~~~~~~~~~~~~~

"Sometimes the REAL reason someone is throwing a lot of mud at you is because they're trying to get rid of some of their OWN!"

~~~~~~~~~~~~~~~~~~~~~~

"Grief stops your life for awhile; but helps you to go on living."

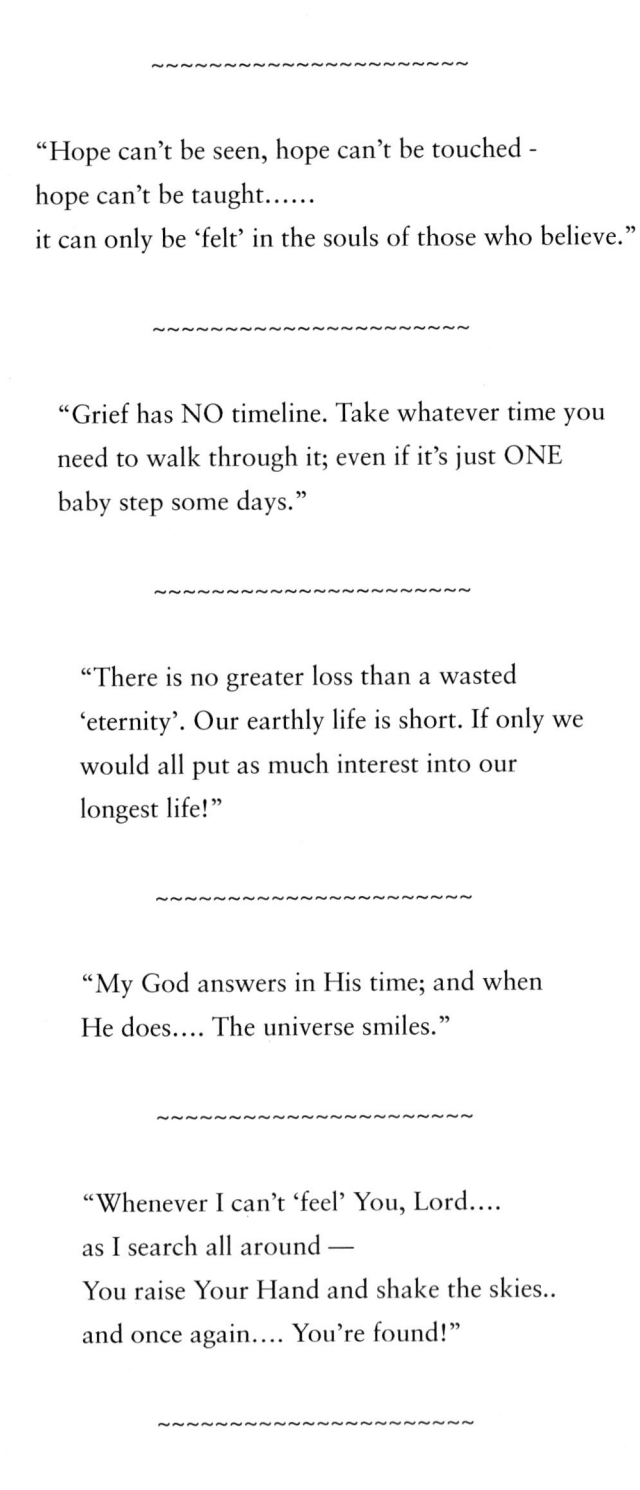

~~~~~~~~~~~~~~~~~~~~~~~

"Hope can't be seen, hope can't be touched -
hope can't be taught……
it can only be 'felt' in the souls of those who believe."

~~~~~~~~~~~~~~~~~~~~~~~

"Grief has NO timeline. Take whatever time you need to walk through it; even if it's just ONE baby step some days."

~~~~~~~~~~~~~~~~~~~~~~~

"There is no greater loss than a wasted 'eternity'. Our earthly life is short. If only we would all put as much interest into our longest life!"

~~~~~~~~~~~~~~~~~~~~~~~

"My God answers in His time; and when He does…. The universe smiles."

~~~~~~~~~~~~~~~~~~~~~~~

"Whenever I can't 'feel' You, Lord….
as I search all around —
You raise Your Hand and shake the skies..
and once again…. You're found!"

~~~~~~~~~~~~~~~~~~~~~~~

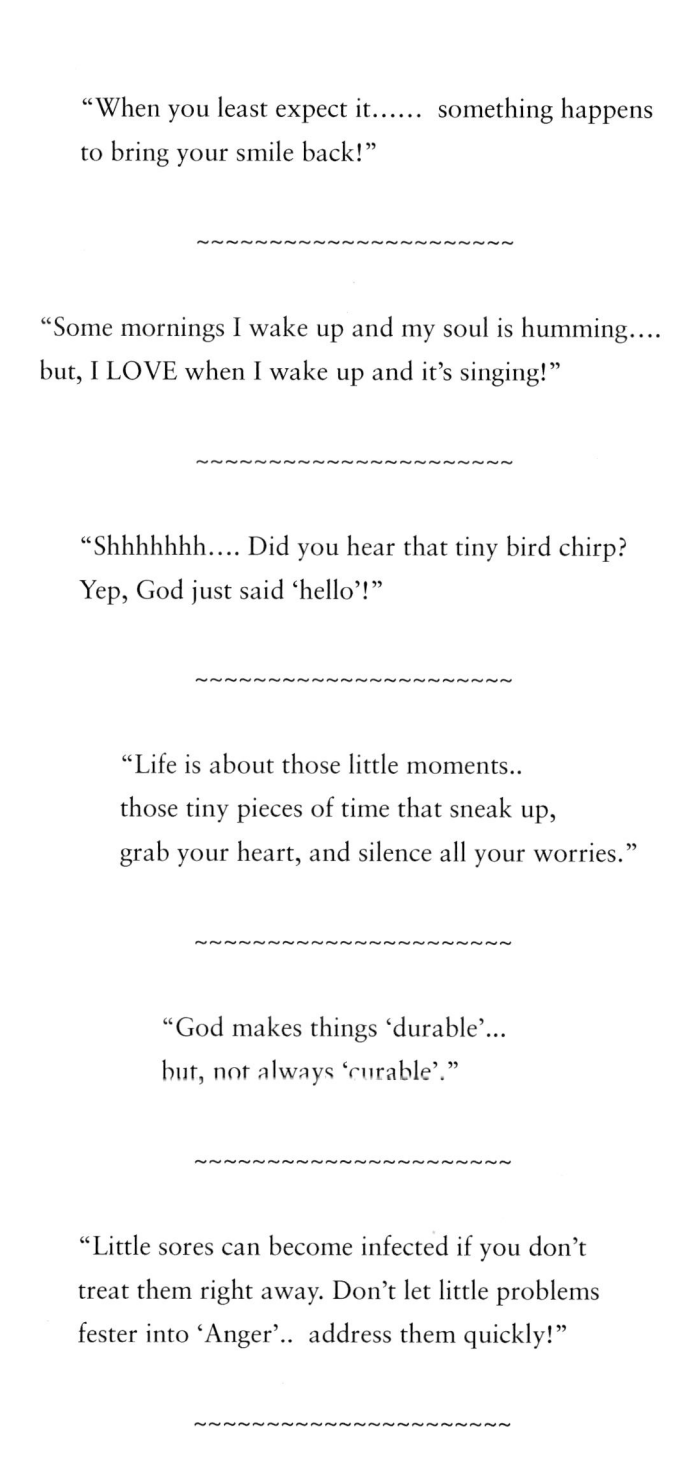

"When you least expect it…… something happens to bring your smile back!"

~~~~~~~~~~~~~~~~~~~~~~

"Some mornings I wake up and my soul is humming…. but, I LOVE when I wake up and it's singing!"

~~~~~~~~~~~~~~~~~~~~~~

"Shhhhhhh…. Did you hear that tiny bird chirp? Yep, God just said 'hello'!"

~~~~~~~~~~~~~~~~~~~~~~

"Life is about those little moments..
those tiny pieces of time that sneak up,
grab your heart, and silence all your worries."

~~~~~~~~~~~~~~~~~~~~~~

"God makes things 'durable'…
but, not always 'curable'."

~~~~~~~~~~~~~~~~~~~~~~

"Little sores can become infected if you don't treat them right away. Don't let little problems fester into 'Anger'.. address them quickly!"

~~~~~~~~~~~~~~~~~~~~~~

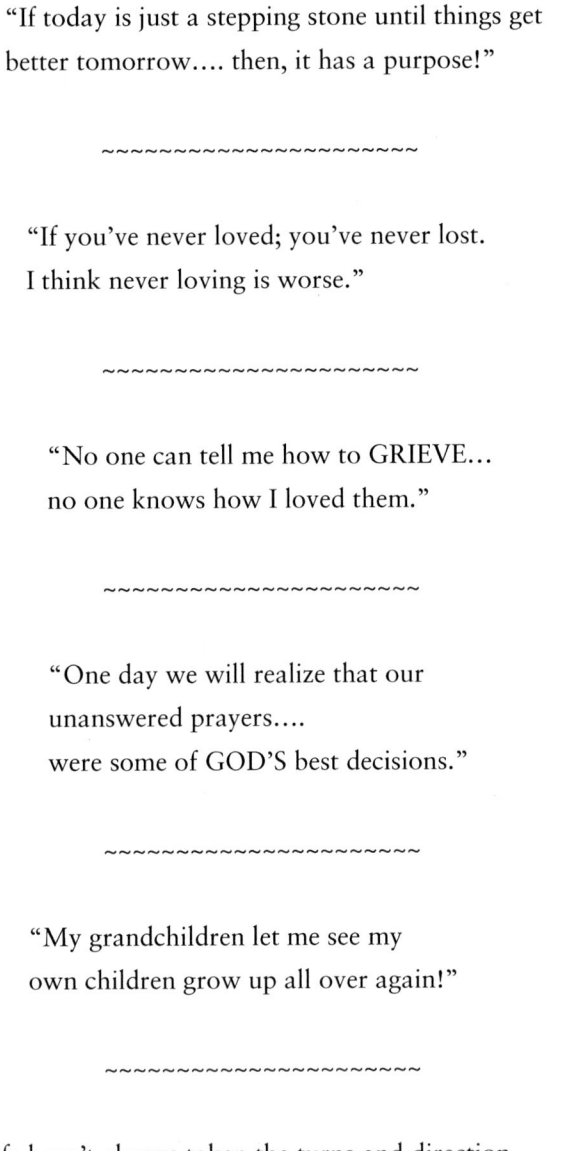

"If today is just a stepping stone until things get better tomorrow…. then, it has a purpose!"

~~~~~~~~~~~~~~~~~~~~

"If you've never loved; you've never lost.
I think never loving is worse."

~~~~~~~~~~~~~~~~~~~~

"No one can tell me how to GRIEVE…
no one knows how I loved them."

~~~~~~~~~~~~~~~~~~~~

"One day we will realize that our
unanswered prayers….
were some of GOD'S best decisions."

~~~~~~~~~~~~~~~~~~~~

"My grandchildren let me see my
own children grow up all over again!"

~~~~~~~~~~~~~~~~~~~~

"My life hasn't always taken the turns and direction
that I've wished it had. I've been stopped, detoured, and lost.
The ride's not always fun —- but, the destination will be
worth it!!!!"

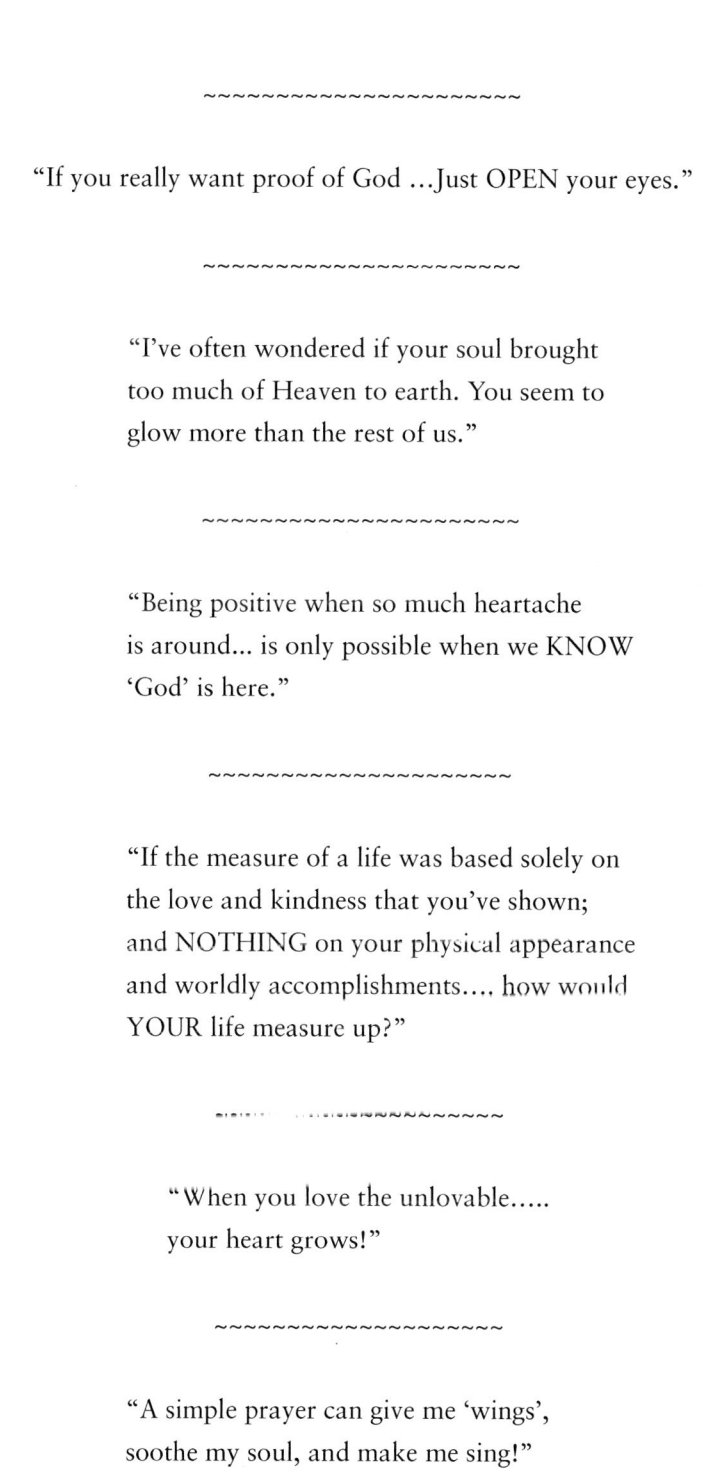

~~~~~~~~~~~~~~~~~~~~~~

"If you really want proof of God …Just OPEN your eyes."

~~~~~~~~~~~~~~~~~~~~~~

"I've often wondered if your soul brought too much of Heaven to earth. You seem to glow more than the rest of us."

~~~~~~~~~~~~~~~~~~~~~~

"Being positive when so much heartache is around… is only possible when we KNOW 'God' is here."

~~~~~~~~~~~~~~~~~~~~~~

"If the measure of a life was based solely on the love and kindness that you've shown; and NOTHING on your physical appearance and worldly accomplishments…. how would YOUR life measure up?"

~~~~~~~~~~~~~~~~~~~~~~

"When you love the unlovable….. your heart grows!"

~~~~~~~~~~~~~~~~~~~~~~

"A simple prayer can give me 'wings', soothe my soul, and make me sing!"

~~~~~~~~~~~~~~~~~~~

"Dear moonit beams of softened light ~
lay tight around my room tonight. And
may my spirit dance within… until the
sun comes up again."

~~~~~~~~~~~~~~~~~~~

"The years move on so quickly….
I blinked, and they flew by.
I always heard that LOVE'S what counts -
and now can cherish why."

~~~~~~~~~~~~~~~~~~~

"Losing a child can only be compared
to….
NOTHING ELSE."

~~~~~~~~~~~~~~~~~~~

"Jesus is my GARMIN….
He guides me home."

~~~~~~~~~~~~~~~~~~~

"I have 'lost' in almost every way; yet,
I am blessed beyond measure….
that's what GOD can do!"

~~~~~~~~~~~~~~~~~

"Only with constant practice can we give
our worries to God. Our brains are trained
to take them back."

~~~~~~~~~~~~~~~~~

"This storm is bigger than the rest -
in power, strength, and fear.
But, through the dark hours of this test....
I KNOW my God is here."

~~~~~~~~~~~~~~~~~

"Twinkling stars that glow up high...
fill our silent, darkened sky.
May each one send dreams of peace;
and fill your heart with sweet release."

~~~~~~~~~~~~~~~~~

"The dawn sings out His glory...
each hour displays His light.
Although I see God everywhere...
I see Him most at night."

~~~~~~~~~~~~~~~~~

"Only with sorrows are new joys sought."

~~~~~~~~~~~~~~~~~

"The only place I know to go right now....
is to my KNEES."

~~~~~~~~~~~~~~~~~

"A baby still has Heaven in it's eyes -
just take a deep look."

~~~~~~~~~~~~~~~~~

"May every moment whisper a soft
breeze of 'hello'. I pray your heart be
touched by God, wherever you may go."

~~~~~~~~~~~~~~~~~

"Each of us has inherited the strength to
overcome, the ability to forgive,
and the desire to love ——
    just look who our 'Father' is!"

~~~~~~~~~~~~~~~~~

"Perhaps God allows those last painful days to continue…
NOT for the one who is suffering; but, to show others
the strength FAITH provides."

~~~~~~~~~~~~~~~~~~~

"May angels flutter near you,
and coat you with their wings.

May sweet dreams fill your sleeping…
until the morning sings!"

~~~~~~~~~~~~~~~~~~~

"Our earthly heart reminds us from time
to time that it's broken."

~~~~~~~~~~~~~~~~~~~

"How softly comes the night - in silence barely heard;
how tender come the stars - without a single word..
yet, in such subtle motion, the world appears as new;
as countless golden moonbeams reach down to cover you."

~~~~~~~~~~~~~~~~~~~

"That tiny whisper to God in the morning
echoes through Heaven like a song!"

~~~~~~~~~~~~~~~~~~~

"Only God knows which way the wind blows…..
it's HIS breath."

~~~~~~~~~~~~~~~~~~~

"Sometimes God talks to me all day……and He hasn't said a word."

~~~~~~~~~~~~~~~~~~~

"There is NO ending to an eternal story."

~~~~~~~~~~~~~~~~~~~~

"Oh, how soft the evening breaks;
when every creature starts to make…
a tender bed for it to rest ~~
oh, how I love the evenings best!"

~~~~~~~~~~~~~~~~~~~~

"If you keep your eyes looking toward the light;
you won't notice the darkness as much."

~~~~~~~~~~~~~~~~~~~~

"I asked God if I could 'feel' Him;
He said, 'Just Breathe'."

~~~~~~~~~~~~~~~~~~~~

"Love can never hurt more than it has helped….
a soul must always remember that."

~~~~~~~~~~~~~~~~~~~~

"Sometimes you can still smell the scent of
Heaven on a newborn baby."

~~~~~~~~~~~~~~~~~~~~

"How can anyone believe our galaxy is
just a coincidence? Who amongst us can
even imagine it's precision!"

~~~~~~~~~~~~~~~~~~~~

"Every minute that goes by…
I'm sixty seconds closer to Heaven!"

~~~~~~~~~~~~~~~~~~~~

"Some days all you can do is breathe
through them. It's okay. God Understands."

~~~~~~~~~~~~~~~~~~~~

"There is no sadder ending to a life
than an empty soul."

~~~~~~~~~~~~~~~~~~~~

"In Heaven there is no need to dream…..
they have all come true!"

~~~~~~~~~~~~~~~~~~~~

"The swaying of a tree's branches is just one
of God's lullabies."

~~~~~~~~~~~~~~~~~~~~

"Don't ever waste of moment of your vision….
use it to truly 'see'."

~~~~~~~~~~~~~~~~~~~~

"Prayer allows your sleep to bless you."

~~~~~~~~~~~~~~~~~~~

"Take my soul Lord ... and wrap Your Strength around it ~ lest I get tired."

~~~~~~~~~~~~~~~~~~~

Epilogue

I hope that these works of poetry will continue to help you through every trial that comes your way. Losing someone is always so hard but the wonderful memories that you will always store in your heart are worth the pain. There are so many signs of beauty in this world to show us that God is ever present.

I hope that everyone can feel the beauty that God has given us in the poems that talk of His incredible miracles of nature! I believe that Heaven will far outweigh the most beautiful sights that we all experience here on 'Earth'.

Thank you to all my family and friends who have been there for ME whenever I needed them. Love to everyone who has encouraged me along the way. Each of you are priceless.

A special thank you to Michael Frank of Tiffin, Ohio for being an objective eye and reading through all of my poetry to check on spelling and errors. He has been an incredible support to me as I wrote the poems contained in this book.

God Bless,

Diane Ranker Riesen